# John Updike's *Rabbit at Rest*

# Modern American Literature
## New Approaches

Yoshinobu Hakutani
*General Editor*

Vol. 18

PETER LANG
New York • Washington, D.C./Baltimore • Boston
Bern • Frankfurt am Main • Berlin • Vienna • Paris

Dilvo I. Ristoff

# John Updike's *Rabbit at Rest*

## Appropriating History

PETER LANG
New York • Washington, D.C./Baltimore • Boston
Bern • Frankfurt am Main • Berlin • Vienna • Paris

**Library of Congress Cataloging-in-Publication Data**

Ristoff, Dilvo I.
John Updike's Rabbit at rest: appropriating history / Dilvo I. Ristoff.
p. cm. — (Modern American literature; vol. 18)
Includes bibliographical references and index.
1. Updike, John, Rabbit at rest. 2. Literature and history—United States—History—
20th century. 3. Historical fiction, American—History and criticism. 4. Updike,
John—Characters—Harry Angstrom. 5. Angstrom, Harry (Fictitious character).
6. Nineteen eighties. I. Title. II. Series: Modern American literature
(New York, N.Y.); vol. 18.
PS3571.P4R2337 813'.54—dc21 98–4813
ISBN 0-8204-3990-8
ISSN 1078-0521


**Die Deutsche Bibliothek-CIP-Einheitsaufnahme**

Ristoff, Dilvo I.:
John Updike's Rabbit at rest: appropriating history / Dilvo I. Ristoff.
–New York; Washington, D.C./Baltimore; Boston; Bern; Frankfurt am Main;
Berlin; Vienna; Paris: Lang.
(Modern American literature; Vol. 18)
ISBN 0-8204-3990-8

From *Rabbit at Rest* by John Updike Copyright © 1990 by John Updike.
Reprinted by permission of Alfred A. Knopf Inc.

Cover design by James F. Brisson
Cover Art: O Livro da Criação Latinoamericana (detail). Artist: Rodrigo de Haro.

The paper in this book meets the guidelines for permanence and durability
of the Committee on Production Guidelines for Book Longevity
of the Council of Library Resources.

*To my wife*

MARIA

*and*

*my daughter*

CLARISSA

The choice of his subject, and the manner of treating it, depended not alone on his individual will. It was given him by the belief in which he had been brought up, the education which he received, the spirit, habits, beliefs, prejudices, tastes, cravings of the age and country in which he lived, or for which he sang.

—Orestes A. Brownson, "Emerson"

The historical narrative does not reproduce the events it describes; it tells us in what direction to think about the events.

—Hayden White, *Tropics of Discourse*

# ABBREVIATIONS

| | |
|---|---|
| CABG | Coronary Artery Bypass Graft |
| FA | Farewell Address |
| FDA | Food and Drug Administration |
| HD | *Historic Documents* |
| HUD | Housing and Urban Development |
| MI | Miocardiac Infarction |
| MODERN | *Modern Fiction Studies* |
| NOW | National Organization for Women |
| NYT | *The New York Times* |
| PP | *Picked-up Pieces* |
| PRIME | *Primetime Live* |
| PTL | Praise the Lord |
| RA | *Rabbit Angstrom* |
| RRE | *Rabbit Redux* |
| RICH | *Rabbit Is Rich* |
| SC | *Self-Consciousness* |
| S and L | Savings and Loan |
| TD | *Tropics of Discourse* |
| TNIA | *Television News Index Abstract* |
| WEEK | *This Week* with David Brinkley |

# CONTENTS

# PREFACE

In December 1987 I had the privilege of a brief encounter with John Updike. It was a very cold and sunny Sunday morning, and in Beverly Farms, Massachusetts, where he lived then and still lives today, crowds of people were gathered around the local churches. As a result (or was it because of his critics?), when I met him at a street corner the first question that came to my mind was "Are you going to church?" He told me that no, he was *coming* from church and going to the drugstore to buy a newspaper. He bought the *Boston Globe,* and we drove to his home, only a few minutes from downtown.

It was there and then that I took the picture of Updike which I believe is emblematic of my way of reading his work. The picture shows Updike, in hat and overcoat, standing on the neatly mowed lawn in front of his home—a majestic house surrounded with Greek columns—holding the *Boston Globe* in his hand. It is my conviction that this is precisely how John Updike should be "seen"; that is, less as somebody holding a Bible in his hand and more as somebody holding a newspaper, less as somebody on his way to church and more as somebody on his way home to read the newspaper, less as somebody concerned with the other-worldly or transcendental and more as somebody in love with the "daily doings of ordinary people."

The picture also expresses my conviction that Updike is an author who holds the information of the media close to himself at all times, and he carries it with him into his home, his workplace, and his fiction. His work should, thus, preferably be read along with the texturizations which the newspapers and the media as a whole make of American life. On every page of each of his novels, we are explicitly invited to historicize and to perceive that the American scene is not only a *locus* but a *motive* for the characters' actions. As Updike himself puts it, "My fiction about the daily doings of ordinary people has more history in it than history books . . . in each of my novels, a precise year is given and a President reigns; *The Centaur* is distinctly a Truman book, and *Rabbit, Run* an Eisenhower one. *Couples* could only have taken place under Kennedy" (Plath 37). And we could add: *Rabbit Redux* is a book of the Nixon era; *Rabbit Is Rich*, of the Carter era; and *Rabbit at Rest*, of the "reigns" of Reagan and Bush (not to mention *Memories of the Ford Administration*, which is Updike's satire on a president who doesn't seem to have existed).

Accordingly Updike is today's great chronicler of the American life which started gaining sharpness of definition in the 1950s. This life is most clearly depicted in his most widely acclaimed body of work, the Rabbit tetralogy: *Rabbit, Run* (1960), *Rabbit Redux* (1971), *Rabbit Is Rich* (1981), and *Rabbit at Rest* (1990). These novels portray the life of white, Anglo-Saxon Protestant Harry (Rabbit) Angstrom during the fifties, sixties, seventies, and eighties. Rabbit is revisited at the end of each decade as Updike leads him to confront the major issues of his day and place. Although at times shockingly honest and highly sensitive and human, Rabbit is not always a likable character. His treatment of communists, foreigners, blacks, women, and gays often brings him close to the belligerent anticommunist, the angry nationalist, and the phallocentric racist. It is, however, precisely Rabbit's ambiguity which,

combined with Updike's stylistic virtuosity and masterful depiction of everyday life, has been the object of continuous admiration of readers and critics alike.

Described in *Rabbit at Rest* as "the still center" around which
the world is gaseous and undefined, Rabbit becomes the point of
encounter for the forces of change. Fearful and doubtful of the
legitimacy of the cries of protest he hears all around him, Updike's hero becomes the tireless "devourer" of news, newness,
and otherness—somebody permanently engaged in the attempt to
bring the most diverse, the most extreme and marginal to the safe
limits of middleness.

The referentiality of Updike's text is such that it is easy to
perceive that the relations and conflicts within it are directly
generated by the historic texturizations produced by the media,
frequently by events of national and international impact. In the
fifties, the Cold War, the Korean War, the Dalai Lama's escape
from Tibet during the Chinese invasion of 1959, the arrival of
television as the new American baby-sitter, and the web of
highways from the Eisenhower era leave Rabbit confused,
without destiny, and unable to take upon himself the
responsibility of adult life, just as his country is still uncertain
about the demands of its new role as world leader. In the sixties,
the Vietnam War, the Civil Rights movement, the hippie
movement, the trip to the moon, and Ted Kennedy's car accident
in Chappaquidick are all events which, quite literally, set Rabbit's
home on fire. In the seventies, the oil embargo, the long lines at
the gas stations, the invasion of the little gas-saving Toyotas in the
American automobile market, and the hostage crisis in Iran create
a Rabbit who shares the same crisis of confidence as his president.
Most recently, in the eighties, the end of the Cold War, the AIDS
epidemic and its effects on sexual behavior, the war on drugs, the
international debt crisis, the budget and trade deficits, the effects

of Reaganomics, the Japanese economic invasion, the destabilizing forces of feminism, and the explosion of PanAm flight 103 over Scotland leave Rabbit with a sense that his days are over and that death is now the only thing he can count on. The thoughts, the moods, and the actions of the story are one with the daily events and circumstances of a particular people in a particular time and place, constituting the body and soul of Updike's fiction.

The celebration of "the glory of the daily," however, does not only mean having to overlook the deeds of the great heroes and villains and to privilege the doings of common mortals; it means also a perception of common people as translators of moments which marked their lives and the life of their country. For the theorizers and political analysts, the end of the Cold War may have signified the debacle of a certain model of social organization, a crucial moment of rupture in the relations between world powers, or even, as for Francis Fukuyama, the end of history. For Updike's hero, the common citizen who for decades has consumed the anticommunist ideology as the most appetizing dish on the menu, the moment means simply a major loss of purpose in life. When Reagan and Gorbachev start "getting cozy" in 1988, Harry Angstrom asks himself, "Without the cold war, what is the purpose of being an American?" Robbed of his objective in life, he no longer finds a reason to get up in the morning.

It is from these popular appropriations of historical events and circumstances that Updike constructs his fiction—so close to daily life, so close to the newspaper which he carries with him, that the frontiers of fact and fiction, history and story, become tenuous and difficult to distinguish. Thanks to this way of translating the world, the unheroic heroes of Updike receive the breath of life; serve as pretext to celebrate the common, with all its virtues and vices; and give back to history, through story, the life they have acquired.

This book is a sequel to my *Updike's America*, published in 1988. Although the method is the same, my conclusion shows that upon closer reading we perceive that Updike's proximity to the media and his appropriation of history are even greater than originally thought. The actions of *Rabbit at Rest* follow such a remarkable day-to-day synchrony that not only its themes but also the metaphors the characters construct, in many instances, come straight out of newspapers or daily television news broadcasts. Rabbit is "history," not only because he embraces the ideology of a decade that is long over but also because he absorbs and tries to find meaning in the world that Tom Brokaw, Dan Rather, Peter Jennings, and the media present to him while more history is in the making.

I am grateful to all those colleagues and friends who have read the manuscript and made valuable suggestions for its improvement. My special gratitude to Professor Townsend Ludington for his generous and professional advice, to Charlotte Pence for her patient revisions of the manuscript, and to reference librarian Thomas Nixon, from the University of North Carolina's Davis Library, for his valuable assistance in locating the many resources which undergird the following discussion. I thank also the CAPES Foundation for a fellowship during which this work was completed.

Dilvo I. Ristoff
November 1997

# INTRODUCTION

Out of soiled and restless life, I have refined my books.

—John Updike, *Self-Consciousness*

At age sixty-five John Updike continues to be as productive as he was at the beginning of his career forty-three years ago. His short stories, chronicles, poems, novels, and reviews continue to show up in the *New Yorker* and other journals and magazines throughout the United States and the world. And for those who thought that he was running out of gas, a surprise: Alfred Knopf has just published Updike's latest novel, *Toward the End of Time*— a novel as rich, imaginative, and well-crafted as the best in contemporary American fiction.

Where does this productive capacity come from? Without trying to downplay his creativity, undeniably it has more to do with perspiration than with the muses. Updike writes religiously every day of the year, and his day only ends when at least three pages of text have been produced. This seminarian's self-discipline is what assures him that at the end of each year, additions and subtractions made, he has at least two respectable volumes on the market.

Or almost that. Since 1954, when he graduated from Harvard University with the *summa cum laude* distinction in English and

decided to earn a living as a writer, Updike has published exactly
seventy volumes, including seventeen novels, various collections
of short stories, several volumes of poetry, a large number of
reviews, and numerous pieces of literary criticism.[1] In all of these
genres he has been successful. For his poetry he was given
coveted literary prizes in the United States and Great Britain; for
his short stories, besides half a dozen other prizes, he received the
National Book Award; for his novels he was distinguished once
more with the National Book Award, two Pulitzer Prizes, and
numerous other prizes; and for his work in literary criticism he
was honored with the National Book Critics Circle Award. As his
most prominent critic, Donald Greiner, puts it, "Updike is a
master of four genres" (Giles 252).

At age thirty-five, Updike wrote *Midpoint,* a poetic inventory of
his life up to that moment, imagining that perhaps, with luck, he
would make it to seventy. Judging from the rhythm of his
production and from the energy with which he faces the
intellectual challenges put to him every day, it won't be difficult
at all for him to arrive at seventy. Perhaps he should have written
*Midpoint* at age forty or forty-five. This is also what the French
seem to think—the French who have just honored him with the
title *Commandeur de l'Ordre des Arts et des Lettres.* Despite his gray
hair, wrinkled face, and caramelized skin, John Updike is today
precisely this—the great commander of the arts and letters—a
reason for pride and admiration among lovers of literature
throughout the world.

Updike is not only one of the most prolific and widely read
contemporary fiction writers, he is also simultaneously the most
American and the most universal among them. His text rejects
what Updike calls the traditional "outsiderish literary stance" of
American literature; it is "a ticket to the America all around us"

---

[1] For a complete list of Updike's publications see Appendix 2.

(*RA* ix); it comes with the territory, with time and place, with the cars, the highways, the motels and hotels, the magazines, the snacks, the foods, the ubiquitous shopping places, the ever-present television shows, the films, the popular songs, the beers, the eating places, the painkiller ads—in short, with the scene. This American scene, which is often but not always made of headlines, is appropriated by his protagonists in such a way that their feelings, emotions, and dramas are always more than their own, more than American. As Donald Greiner notes, although "a reader would be hard-pressed to name a contemporary author other than John Updike who is more in tune with the way most Americans live . . . he probes the crises that sear the *human* spirit" (Giles 252, my emphasis).

My earlier book, *Updike's America* (1988), is a discussion of the use of contemporary American history in what was then Updike's Rabbit trilogy. Briefly put, my argument in that book is that Updike's fiction grows out of the history in which it is inserted, out of what we may call the American scene, and *not* out of Rabbit's idiosyncrasies and freakish wishes. The inference was born in the observation that Updike's fiction, with its great concern for time and space and all the memorabilia that go along with them, is incessantly and even obsessively referential in nature.

This referentiality makes the social relations and conflicts of the novels' characters directly generated by history, often by events of national and international repercussion (e.g., the Cold War, the Korean War, the Vietnam War, the Civil Rights movement, the hippie movement, man's trip to the moon, Ted Kennedy's car accident in Chappaquidick, the 1979 oil crisis and Iranian hostage crisis, the invasion of the United States by Japanese businesses and money, the falling of the space lab, the crisis of confidence of the Carter era, the Iranian revolution, etc.), so that the Rabbit novels are indeed to a large extent, as Updike puts it, "a kind of running report on the state of [Harry Angstrom] and his nation" (*RA* ix).

My view, therefore, is that Updike's hero—the middle American—is moved much more by historical events, by what happens *to* him, than by what he makes happen, although the nature of what happens to him seems to become relevant only because of a preexisting historical-fictional kinship. We might think of Herodotus telling us to "remember that men are dependent on circumstances, and not circumstances on men," as Updike himself reminds us in the epigraph of *Rabbit, Run*: No matter how graceful our motions, there are always "external circumstances" to press upon them. Rabbit is, in fact, so deeply involved in and carried along by these events and circumstances that compose the scene of the fifties, sixties, seventies, and eighties that he lacks the distance to fully understand them. And because he cannot fully understand them, he struggles against the impossibility of declaring himself the master of his own destiny. The speed with which changes occur in his highly mobile and event-prone country makes Rabbit a man in constant conflict with his milieu, even when his wish is to conform.

I also argued in 1988 that the Rabbit novels could be consistently read, from the first to the last, with a scene-centered approach, thus preserving Rabbit's fundamental ideological characteristics—the characteristics of the "middle American radical" as defined by Donald I. Warren in his book, *The Radical Center* (1976). Warren identifies these characteristics as being militarism, racism, nationalism, religiosity, and authoritarianism. Depending on the realm in which we choose to concentrate our attention, we may add individualism, anticommunism, and sexism to this list.

The scene-centered approach allows us to see that Rabbit invariably stands with those forces of middle America which, as a rule, have been hegemonic since the 1950s. But because the always active antagonistic forces need to be absorbed or co-opted by the system, and because power changes hands and styles and people are replaced, Rabbit is intermittently pushed into crises and forced to renegotiate his relationship with his country. In his present, he seems to be always already a prisoner of a nostalgic pull that brings to his mind images of a world that is grander and better, more glorious and more desirable than the drudgery and turmoil he now faces. As Malcolm Cowley once put it, "A man rising in the world is not concerned with history; he is too busy making it. But a citizen with a fixed place in the community wants to acquire a glorious past just as he acquires antique furniture. By that past he is reassured of his present importance; in it he finds strength to face the dangers that lie in front of him" (Carper 76). Similarly Rabbit, the common citizen, will feed on the appreciation shown by some of his townspeople during the Fourth of July parade; he will need to mention his past feats to his Jewish friends, read into every event and circumstance the accumulated experiences of his life, and exhibit as a trophy the newspaper clippings that tell the world of his past glory. For the same reason, he will follow closely all major events related to his country— political, social, economic, cultural, athletic—and he will always, because of his essentially conservative nature, identify more closely with the president who has just left office, or is about to leave it, than he does with the president in office, or about to be inaugurated. For each president, as for each decade, a new process of readaptation is required. This process is a major source of conflict and tension in the Rabbit novels.

Rabbit's impulsive, instinctive, and reactive rather than planned response to the world requires an analytical approach which is scene-centered—an approach which regards scene not only as a *locus* for actions but also as the *motive* for actions. As I argued in *Updike's America*, "only a scene-centered approach . . .

can account for the fundamental tensions in the Rabbit trilogy, for Harry Angstrom is much too static, anti-intellectual, and anti-problematic a character to be able to generate by himself significant conflicts. These are always primarily scene-centered and only then do we see them in connection to the agent, purpose, and agency" (9). The same, I believe, can be said of *Rabbit at Rest*.

The scene-centered reading of the first three Rabbit novels was necessary in 1988 because of the possibilities it opened for us to see, as one reviewer noted in *Modern Fiction Studies*, "how historically representative Rabbit in fact is" (771). Donald Greiner, Robert Detweiler, Suzanne Uphaus, Charles Berryman, Anthony Quinton, and others had already pointed out the importance of history in Updike's novels, but no in-depth study had yet been made to disclose "the variety of ways political and social events are . . . reflected [and illumined] in the novels" (*Modern* 771). Although this kind of reading is still held at arm's length in certain academic circles, more and more of Updike's critics stress the presence of the historical scene in his fiction. Stewart Sanderson claims that "the bleak conclusion [in *Rabbit at Rest*] is reinforced by images of national decline in the years of Reaganomics. Rabbit and his country are one" (Henderson 55). Similarly Stacey Olster argues that "the America that Harry Angstrom is meant to mirror is in steady decline in Updike's novels" (*Modern* 46). Even critics like Raymond A. Mazureck, Jan Clausen, and others who clearly dislike Updike's Rabbit admit that Updike deals extensively with historical forces in his fiction, although Clausen would call it "sporting with history" (*Kenyon* 47), and Mazureck would say that Updike's history is too superficial to successfully explain what postwar America was like (Sorkin 144). In other words, even where there is clear disagreement as to the degree of success of Updike's use of history, there is always an underlying affirmation of its presence.

With the publication of *Rabbit at Rest* in 1990 the Rabbit trilogy became a tetralogy, Updike declared the Harry Angstrom saga concluded, and *Updike's America* became incomplete, requiring me to expand the study. The present text is thus a natural outgrowth of *Updike's America*, and its purpose is to show how Updike's hero copes with the new destabilizing forces which overwhelm him in the 1980s.

The methodology is the same used to analyze the first three novels. The approach, which I call "scene-centered," is greatly indebted to the concepts expounded by Kenneth Burke in *A Grammar of Motives* (1945) and Hayden White in *Metahistory* (1973) and *Tropics of Discourse* (1978). This combination allows us to see not only the forms the textural organization may take but also the predominant centers or locations from which Updike's fiction extracts its energy. Burke's dramatistic perspective, in the various possible combinations of his pentad, and White's self-conscious narrative modes of historical construction bring to the perception of each individual action a salutary consciousness of the arbitrariness of data and the ways we juxtapose them, interpret them, and make them part of our fictions, disclosing scenic dimensions which would otherwise go unnoticed.

Hayden White claims (quite correctly, I believe) that it is not unusual for "literary theorists, when they are speaking about the 'context' of a literary work, to suppose that this context—the historical milieu—has a concreteness and accessibility that the work itself can never have, as if it were easier to perceive the reality of a past world put together from a thousand historical documents than it is to probe the depths of a single literary work that is present to the critic studying it . . ." (*TD* 91). The reality that we apprehend, therefore, if we extend White's reasoning, is always a reduction, an expansion, a restriction and a breaking of borders, a fabrication, a fraction, a view. It is a construct which results from particular combinations of elements and strategies in a complex multidirectional relationship between agents, actions, agencies, scenes, and purposes and which is always loaded with contradictions and torn by fragmentation. It is in the realm of these combinations that we can identify some of White's constructs which constitute the particular readings into reality, or the world of tropes—a world in which "discourse is regarded as an apparatus for the production of meaning rather than only a vehicle for the transmission of information about an extrinsic referent" (*Content* 42).

White defines a trope as a mode of apprehending reality. Trope not only reveals how we go about understanding the world around us but also how we understand our relationship to it. Our mode of apprehension necessarily contaminates discourse and should be identifiable in any kind of discourse, be it historical, literary, or scientific. A narrative is, therefore, never a mere "transposition of facts, but rather a way of telling us how and what we are supposed to think about them." Similarly, "the historical narrative does not reproduce the events it describes; it tells us in what direction to think about the events . . ." (*TD* 91). These events, we should always remember, were accorded the status of "historic" by an always arbitrary, ideologically-oriented, and selective mental process.

White identifies four major forms of apprehending the world: the metaphoric, the metonymical, the synecdochical, and the ironic. Although each of these modes represents a different level of complexity, as if they were stages of human development, individuals tend to produce texts which wander, consciously or unconsciously, from mode to mode in an endless effort to adapt, to grasp, to see, to understand, and to control.

Metaphor is the trope in which the nonfamiliar is viewed in terms of that which is always already familiar. In other words, the world, no matter what it is, can only be that which I conceive it to be. In a way, *my* world is what the world is, or, put differently, *my idea* of the world is what the world is. The new, therefore, is reduced to my limits, the world being unavoidably hedge-clipped into familiarity. In the world of metaphor, in its purest sense, there is no consciousness that the world can exist beyond my idea of it, and if and when circumstances determine this separate existence as an actual possibility, the other is "cannibalized" —disintegrated through integration into the limits of my organism. The metaphorical mind as a consequence tends to perceive its own reproduction or reconstruction of facts as the facts themselves, permanently enslaved by what White calls "the seduction of a world which is nothing but the creation of our longings"—a subjectification carried to the extreme.

In White's view then the metaphor is not merely a comparison of two things on the basis of a shared quality, as we would usually define it. Although he would not deny that comparison is taking place, his emphasis falls on the fact that one of the elements of the comparison always gains precedence over the other. Thus the unfamiliar is made familiar, the external is made internal, the other is made me, the foreign is made national, the different is made same, the margin is made center. In metaphor there is always a hardening of a core which functions as a point of reference, a *point d'apuis*, and is always more memory than desire, more remembering than forgetting.

Updike's Rabbit, like middle America, has made a living off of familiarizing, co-opting, integrating, and neutralizing antagonistic forces. Blacks, hippies, communists, foreigners, and others—all are systematically reduced to middleness, all are brought down to his limits. In other words, for Rabbit the other or the different only acquires meaning as long as it is comparable to entities whose existence he recognizes. Since this seems to be the way most of us operate in our daily lives, Rabbit becomes in our eyes extremely human, the average citizen, one of us. Metaphor, in its purest sense, is much like Michel Tournier's comments on Robinson Crusoe: "I who do the knowing, the tasting, touching, and cooking have no separate existence except when I perform the act of reflection which causes *me* to emerge—a thing which in fact rarely happens" (230). It is interesting to note that Tournier is extensively quoted by Updike in *Self-Consciousness*.

In metonymy, I and the world are separate and distinct. I am able to analyze the world separate from myself, visualizing its constituents, its parts and their relations. The world, I realize, has its own rules, beyond me, and the parts share a relation of contiguity. Metonymy is thus the analytical, the separate, the scientific—the trope which confirms the possibility of the outside, no matter how central I regard myself or how broadly or narrowly I define my limits.

Rabbit does seem to exhibit some metonymical reasoning when he discusses the events and circumstances around him. Yet the events and circumstances, even in their outsidedness, or in the identifiable congruity and incongruity of their constituents, are always most emphatically discussed in relation to himself, never independently. Thus the explosion of the PanAmerican airplane over Lockerbie, Scotland, brings back the death of baby Becky in the 1950s, and of Jill in the 1960s; Nelson's drug addiction brings back Rabbit's adventure with Skeeter in *Rabbit Redux*; and the victories and the retirement of Mike Schmidt, whose historical significance hardly overcomes the realm of the provincial, only interest him as long as they are a part of or an extension of himself. The same goes for Yogi Berra, Steve Bedrosian, Juan Samuel, Pete Rose, Ivan Lendl, and Martina Navratilova—they interest him only to the extent that they match his appropriation of them, only insofar as they, like himself, are losing and forced to make space for the younger generation. In his synthesis of them, through scenic suggestion, they are made to be like himself, emphatically reinforcing the predominance of the form of metaphorical apprehension.

This brings us to synecdoche, the trope of synthesis. Synecdoche, like metonymy, also implies recognition of the relation of part to whole and may therefore be easily taken as a step beyond metonymy. But synecdoche has as much to do with metaphor as it does with metonymy. What characterizes synecdoche is that it translates apprehension into reduction and ideology. The synecdochic is in fact a particular kind of understanding in which a spiritual characteristic is abstracted from the world. As common examples illustrate, when we say "John is all heart," we do not imagine John is shaped like a heart or that the muscle in his chest is physically representative of him; instead, we imagine John as kind, gentle, and generous. We imagine him having the characteristics which we believe to be associated with the heart, hardly aware that this perception of ours belongs to the realm of constructs or convention rather than to an intrinsic quality of the heart per se. Synecdoche, then, is the realm of the arbitrary and of unavoidably slanted totalizations through which we try not only to perform acts of integration but to make sense of the world. It is the affirmation that the world, chaotic as it may seem, has a meaning—a meaning that may be fixed somehow, through laws, rules, values, and gods.

When we say that Updike's Rabbit appropriates certain events and circumstances synecdochically, we refer to his reading out of these events and circumstances certain ideological or spiritual characteristics which are simultaneously his and middle America's. Paradoxically, reading meaning *out* of the events becomes for Rabbit primarily a reading *into* the events, since his synecdochical perception has its basis more in metaphor than in metonymy, and what he perceives as essential is always what he already knows, having consciously learned it or subliminally acquired it. The vacant space traveled by Voyager 2 becomes, as a consequence, the emptiness of his life, a spiritual emptiness which he is experiencing; the explosion of the PanAm jet is not a technical or a political matter but something mind-boggling, beyond understanding, a feeling of terror which he shares with the nation—a feeling which is not the event, or even a part of it, but one from which we may abstract the universal fear of death.

It is interesting to note that Voyager's journey is perceived by Rabbit's friend Ronnie as a great show of computer graphics—an analytical, metonymical perspective. Accidents like the one at the Sheffield soccer stadium or on the battleship *Iowa* are, for Rabbit's friend Charlie, an unavoidable part of an overcrowded world. For Rabbit, however, these accidents mean that he himself is part of the overcrowding and that soon he will be among the victims. Similarly, kids kissing on the streets mean drugs for Charlie (again an analytical, metonymical apprehension), whereas for Rabbit, whose synecdoches typically go hand in hand with metaphor, the instance becomes immediately ideologized. For Rabbit it means that foreigners are taking over the country and communists and African Americans are plotting to destroy the American way of life, subverting sameness and destabilizing familiarity.

Faced with undeniable historical evidence on the issue, namely Fidel Castro's shipping of common criminals to America a few years earlier, even Charlie has to agree that Rabbit's fear is not totally unjustified. Charlie, however, is after explanations rather than meaning. For him the world is not a mere extension of himself. It has an existence of its own, with its own rules and relationships. Charlie's understanding of the world is based upon explanation—Rabbit's is based upon appropriation.

This leads us to the conclusion that Rabbit, although always grounded in historical evidence, jumps from metaphor to synecdoche without advancing through the metonymical stage. He apprehends synthesis with little or no analysis, which is another way of saying that Rabbit's world is only his to the degree that he has been ideologically construed by and made to identify with the middle American ideology he acquired. Since he, "the solid citizen," hardly ever questions these values or reflects upon their meaning and implications, his life tends to become other-directed and his behavior that of a compulsive "hostage of fortune." As a consequence, Rabbit is dissipated into the public realm of middleness, a space where his ideas cease to be his own and become part of a set repertoire of shared notions, functions, and values to which he is inextricably attached, and which robs him of his individuality.

We should not, therefore, conclude that Rabbit is at a third stage of intellectual performance, having moved beyond metaphor and metonymy. He can never, in fact, cease to be the man in the middle with the ideological characteristics which we have described. Although we may infer that these characteristics belong to him and to his social group, the understanding that these are his characteristics is first Updike's and then the reader's, for Rabbit's understanding of himself as a social phenomenon shows a level of naiveté unmatched by most contemporary literary protagonists. The fact is that Rabbit acts more often than he thinks, and when he does think, he thinks of ways of bringing the larger world into his world, for his is a permanent struggle to make sure that the larger world will not change but adapt.

White's final trope is irony. Irony, as White sees it, is the logical stage per se. Whereas metonymy and synecdoche still require "physical manipulability of the objects," in the ironic stage reasoning can fall on theories and abstractions. This is the stage not only of conscience but of self-consciousness. We may observe and at the same time observe our observations, visualizing our vantage point and defining the structure which guides our observations. The ironic is in some ways, therefore, self-defeating, because it always affirms something which it immediately undermines or denies, not only by pointing toward something other than what it is trying to communicate, but also by pointing to the inability of discourse to fully convey what is meant.

Irony is not Rabbit's form of apprehension, and it is not a dominant characteristic of the tetralogy, for the narrator is much too close to Rabbit to be able to extricate himself from Rabbit's brooding. Underlying the conception of the Rabbit novels, however, is quite obviously the same recontextualization methodology which produced Updike's "Hawthorne" novels: *A Month of Sundays, Roger's Version,* and *S.* Whereas in the Hawthorne novels Updike asks what would Hester Prynne, Roger Chillingworth, and Arthur Dimmesdale be like had they lived in twentieth-century America, in the Rabbit novels Updike is asking what happens to a man, a middle American, as he is compelled decade after decade to face the forces of change.

Updike's fascination with this methodology is also the fascination with the idea of self—something which, bathed by time, is nevertheless able to transcend time and remain identifiable; just as the small-town boy from fictionalized Shillington, Pennsylvania, becomes the mature man of Ipswich, Massachusetts; and as the world-famous writer grows as "things grow, always remembering to be [himself]" (*Rich* 113). In *Self-Consciousness,* Updike cannot help expressing his surprise at discovering that the Shillington he described is not Shillington at all but his version of it, his consciousness of it. Yet, he writes, "isn't it a miracle, the oddity of consciousness being placed in one body rather than another, in one place and not somewhere else, in one handful of decades rather than in ancient Egypt, or ninth-century Wessex, or Samoa before the missionaries came, or Bulgaria under the Turkish yoke, or the Ob River Valley in the day of wooly mammoths? Billions of consciousnesses silt history, and every one of them the center of the universe" (*SC* 40).

Although this particular self-awareness underlies the construction of the Rabbit tetralogy, it is not an object of manipulability of the narrator, as it is, for example, in *Marry Me, Memories of the Ford Administration*, and *Roger's Version*. These novels are much better examples of the ironic trope at work, which is not to say that they are better novels, but that they express very clearly and with great freedom an awareness of their limitations.

The word "scene," it should be emphasized, is used throughout this discussion with the sense it has in Kenneth Burke's *A Grammar of Motives*. It represents a point in time and space *in* which human actions develop and *from* which human agents, agencies, and actions take their energy. The scene is thus not only a *locus* for action but also the major *motive* for actions to occur. Although at times the word comes close to being synonymous with history, and for all practical purposes they are used interchangeably, one should be aware that what is generally regarded as historical narrative is but a very specific texturization or organization of the myriad elements which may constitute the scene. Whereas history tends to texturize topical factual events, the scene may also incorporate the ordinary, the common, the quotidian—ranging from events that make it to the front page of every major newspaper in the country to the memorabilia that constitute what Updike calls "the glory of the daily" and which are not, as a rule, acknowledged by the history books.

Updike expresses his concern about the difference between what we could call historical narratives and scene-centered narratives on several occasions. In *Picked-up Pieces* (1976), he argues that "man is always born into one political contract or another, whose terms, though they sit very lightly at first, eventually, in the form of the draft, or taxes, begin to make heavy demands on you" (*PP* 25). Incapable of escaping the system, an individual's life has to be lived within it, which explains why Updike insists that his books have more history in them than history books. As he sees it, history tends to become lists of major events and dates, deprived of the breath of life. In his autobiographical work, *Self-Consciousness,* and in *Memories of the Ford Administration,* Updike expresses his concern that "the future will forget us, or get us slightly wrong, as our history books get the past wrong, and leave out the very texture of life lived now" (*SC* 257).

What is this texture of life? The memorabilia of a certain time and place, the billboards, the importunities "to buy something" (*SC* 257), television, mail, telephone, paying taxes, driving, "suffering automobile accidents and midnight illnesses and marital discontent" (*SC* 55), listening to music, going to the supermarkets, mating, celebrating birthdays, drinking with friends, invading privacies, going about daily obligations, coming of age and aging, the thrusts, fears, emotions, and dreamings of common individuals—in a word, the scene. This thread of life has been referred to by Updike, in both his fiction and nonfiction, as something ungraspable by history, needing the mediating presence of people, in the middle or in conflict with the middle.

The latest example of his contribution to this discussion comes from *Memories of the Ford Administration* in which the narrator tells his publisher that, having gone over the headlines of the Ford administration days, he came across a long list of deaths. After listing the deaths, he comments: "Surely, *Retrospect* editors, you don't want this sort of thing, which any sophomore with access to a microfilm reader that hasn't broken its fan belt can tote up for you. You want *living* memories and impressions: the untampered-with testimony of those of us fortunate enough to have survived, unlike those named above, the Ford Administration" (6). "Breathing history" is not to be found on lists of wars, deaths, and presidential inaugurations but in the actions of common citizens as they *lived through* these wars, deaths, and inaugurations. However, since topical events do play a major role in the Rabbit novels, "history" and "scene" are sometimes used here as synonyms.

For readers not familiar with *Updike's America*, it might be helpful to recall the four axes which I have argued play a crucial role in the construction of Updike's text: the axis of story, of history, of the memory of the reader, and of the memory of the narrator. These four interconnected axes should help to better visualize the generative forces identified in the novels and the ways they bear upon each other. In that respect, it may be useful to consider a point of intersection between two parallel vertical axes and two parallel horizontal axes, all in direct or indirect connection with each other, and between them a universe which is at once limited and unlimited, a point and a horizon. These axes represent the events and circumstances, the actions and the memories, which populate the Rabbit novels. They tie together story and history in their presentness and throughout time.

One of the vertical axes represents historical events and circumstances, such as the Dalai Lama's escape from the Chinese army in 1959, the trip to the moon in 1969, the Pope's visit to the United States in 1979, or the bombing of the PanAm aircraft over Lockerbie, Scotland, in 1988. On this axis are also various other airplane accidents, the national and international foreign debt crisis, the threat posed by the Japanese economic invasion, the Reagan/Bush war on drugs, the AIDS crisis, the conflict over abortion and women's rights, the retirement of baseball player Mike Schmidt, the expulsion of Pete Rose, the arrest of Yogi Berra's son, and the end of the Cold War, to mention but a few.

The other vertical axis, running parallel but in the opposite direction, to characterize the interconnection, represents the actions of the protagonist. These actions connect with the historical line through the horizontal axes. As examples of this interaction, we could cite Rabbit's actions paralleling those of the Dalai Lama and making him imagine himself the leader of a people, escaping the forces of oppression; or the trip to the moon, stimulating Rabbit to use the astronauts' technical jargon and to see moon imagery all around him, even on his fingernails;[2] we could also mention Rabbit imagining the plane Nelson, Pru, and his grandchildren are on as "a ball of red flame shadowed in black" or "his own death shaped vaguely like an airplane"—most certainly a psychological reaction to the recent Lockerbie tragedy. On the political and economic fronts, we could mention the Brady plan incorporated by Rabbit's son as a strategy for getting out of their financial crisis at the lot or the lack of *giri* (order, responsibility, obligation) as an expression of Japanese interference in domestic affairs. Similarly, on the social side, we could mention the drug problem, the AIDS crisis, the abortion issue, women's activism—all translated into actions as they insinuate themselves or openly exhibit themselves in Rabbit's home during the 1980s.

The third axis, running horizontally from left to right, could be called the reader's memory and participation. The reader remembers, more or less, not only the actions of the characters but also the historical events and scenic circumstances of their time. As Mary O'Connell reminds us when discussing *Rabbit at Rest*, "so much of the novel's pleasure derives from discovering the extent to which we now share Rabbit's memories that it is difficult to imagine how readers unfamiliar with the earlier novels would

---

[2] For an excellent analysis of the use of moon imagery in *Rabbit Redux* see Charles Berryman's "The Education of Harry Angstrom: Rabbit and the Moon" *Literary Review* 27 (1983): 117–126.

respond to *Rabbit at Rest*" (211). And we could add that much of the pleasure derives from knowing the historical events and circumstances which are concomitant with Rabbit's actions in the past and in the present. Since no reader is ideal, that is, no reader fully controls all events in the novel or outside of it, and since no two readers are likely to texturize the historical data in exactly the same way, reader participation and response will vary according to the potential connections made possible through available data and through the tropic imprints he generates as he recollects and reconnects the elements of history and story. Knowing, however, the political and juridical circumstances surrounding Ollie North's activities in the 1980s, for example, we are forced to read and understand Rabbit's concern about Lyle's possible shredding of evidence in the context of the Iran-Contra scandal. Only in this way do we come closer to understanding what is transpiring in Rabbit's mind. If he wants to or not, the reader will make the Iran-Contra scandal part of the story and, along with it, the president's involvement in fighting the Sandinistas in Nicaragua and the communists throughout the world. Rabbit's sentence telling Janice "they'll shred everything like Ollie North" is historically situated, and readers are, if not explicitly asked, then at least encouraged by Updike to historicize.

The same may be said about Voyager 2. Voyager 2 leaves the solar system on August 27, 1989, when Rabbit and Ronnie are playing golf. Knowing that scientists have that same day discovered an immense field of void beyond our galaxy, a well-informed reader will certainly, willing or unwillingly, read into the story not only the historical importance of the event but also Voyager's potential metaphors as it sails forever, without destiny, into the void and the unknown. The image of the void that sickens Rabbit and that is perceived by Ronnie as the mere professional work of computer graphics invites us to read the idea of the void brought by the historical event into the void of Rabbit's present life.

The two different readings that Rabbit and Ronnie produce of Voyager 2's journey past Neptune and into the void may very well be taken as an example of differing reader participation in the world of the story. The difference in their interpretations illustrates not only that readers familiar with the historical events referred to in the novel will produce, to use Stephen Greenblatt's expression, "a set of manipulations" if not better than, then at least different from those produced by less well-informed readers, but it also shows that the *forms* of apprehension are essential for the final imprint of meaning. Although I would argue without hesitation that a well-informed reader will, as a rule, produce manipulations which are more in tune with John Updike's appropriation of the media's historical concerns, and as a consequence, readings which are more easily negotiable in the market of readers and interpreters, it is impossible to escape what by now has become a truism, namely that evident constraints are imposed on facts and events by our modes of apprehension and emplotment; or, put differently, that meaning is produced by the ways individuals or groups construe what they find.

The fourth axis, running horizontally from right to left and completing the intersection, stands for the memory and participation of the narrator. He recreates the characters, placing them in a new historical moment and taking into account what he remembers of their past actions and of the set of values which is at the basis of their behavior. Thus he recreates Rabbit, situating him in a new scene and having him face new characters, always, however, remembering what has already been done and what has already happened and what is or what is not adequate, probable, coherent, or consistent with the foregoing. Rabbit's past—the women he had sex with, the public places, the buildings, the songs, his school, his coach, the political leaders of the country since the 1950s—is an inescapable reference for his present, at times a nightmare. It is not surprising that he drives around Brewer "freshening his memory and hurting himself with the pieces of his old self that cling to almost every corner of the Brewer area" (181). Rabbit's journey follows the path determined by the demands of narratorial memory.

The narrator's memory, as a necessarily historical voice, determines the choice of certain events and circumstances over others, especially when the plausible behavior of the protagonist finds in the historical scene suggestions of something which may enhance or amplify the meaning of his actions. Unless one sees the work of art as a work of chance or haphazard, one cannot help perceive as extremely meaningful the remarkable coincidence, for example, between Jimmy Carter's crisis with the "kids" who hold him "hostage," so to speak, in Iran and Rabbit's crisis with his son Nelson, of whom Rabbit also feels himself a hostage. Rabbit's "running out of gas" at the beginning of *Rabbit Is Rich* parallels the 1979 oil crisis and is just another example of narratorial tropic determination bringing history into fiction and making fiction extrapolate its own realm by making Rabbit's story *mean* more and *be* more than his own.

Since the narrator of *Rabbit at Rest* operates most of the time from within Rabbit's mind, omnisciently reporting everything that Rabbit feels or thinks, it is impossible, most of the time, to distinguish between the two, so that Rabbit's reading of the scene and the narrator's reporting of Rabbit's reading are one and the same. This also means that Rabbit's preferences, choices, and associations are also largely the narrator's, although not necessarily Updike's. Evidence found in the manuscripts shows that Updike actually had to do a significant amount of rewriting in order to make his protagonist and narrator less intellectual and knowledgeable. In many respects, however, Updike admits that his hero is much like himself, sharing, among so many other things, the same "sort of scruffy, flippant patriotism" (Williams 11).

Although it is true that the narrator of *Rabbit at Rest* shows strong attachment to the metaphoric trope in his perception of Rabbit's story (i.e., the Rabbit of the eighties is the Rabbit of the fifties plus the experience of subsequent decades; Rabbit's life is like the life of his leaders and the solid citizens who consider themselves to be led by the same leaders; history is a lot like story and vice versa, etc.), it is also true that construing the new Rabbit, the Rabbit of the eighties, involves as much forgetting as it does remembering. Intentional or unintentional selectivity and exclusion play an important role in reaffirming Rabbit's identity decade after decade.

These four axes, each of which should in fact be represented by double lines in order to stress the ever-present antagonisms in every act and fact,[3] shall direct my analysis of *Rabbit at Rest*. As these axes are bombarded from all sides by ideological forces which manifest themselves in Rabbit's world, the frontier demarcating history and story seems to become less and less easy to identify. Rabbit's story grows out of the American scene just as much as the American scene has been selectively construed to suit Rabbit's story.

The four axes are an attempt to define a possible way of looking at the complexity of the negotiation that takes place between scene and story. This negotiation is at times blatantly explicit and at other times needs to be focused upon because we tend to take it for granted. The negotiation that occurs, however, is largely the result of unconscious historical forces which act upon Updike as

---

[3] It is interesting to recall Updike's definition of fact as something which does not have a meaning in itself but which is necessary for the construction of meaning:

they act upon the narrator and upon Rabbit, as if they were rings sticking together through the energy conveyed by a modern American stone of Heraclea. Author and character see what they see because they are who they are, regardless of what they are trying to do. As Updike himself puts it: "We are all creatures of history . . . I was trying to write about the human predicament, but naturally being an American you write with an American accent, as it were" (Trueheart F4).

Finally, the four axes are an attempt to visualize some of the basic tenets of the New Historicism, as presented by H. Aram Veeser, namely that (1) "every expressive act is embedded in a network of material practices" and, therefore, there is no such thing as speech for speech's sake or discourse for discourse's sake. Discourse or language, as an expressive act, is always part of a network of relations (social, economic, cultural, and material); (2) "literary and non-literary texts circulate inseparably," reaching at times a proximity that dissolves their identity and leads to the perception that history and story are part of the same scene—a broad system of relations which contains both versions of reality—history and story; and (3) "no discourse, imaginative or archival, gives access to unchanging truths nor expresses inalterable human nature." In other words, the hardening of certain historical versions as "history itself," typical of deterministic Old Historicism, should not fail to rescue the consciousness of its being a specific domain of interconnections, another version. A quick look at the myriad facts which were not included in the historical or literary narratives of the 1980s will show that absolutizing is itself a version and lacks the consciousness that one version can reign absolute only until another version is construed and juxtaposed with it.

---

"How circumstantial reality is. Facts are like the individual letters, with their spikes and loops and thorns, that make up words" (*SC* 2).

Within the range of possibilities created by the intersection of the axes, I will identify what I have been calling Updike's America and attempt to bring historical considerations to the center stage of analysis. The historical events and circumstances which inhabit the "death-saturated" world of Rabbit in the eighties are different from those of the earlier decades and need to be pointed out, analyzed, and interpreted. *Rabbit at Rest,* like the previous Rabbit novels, contains a version of America which will stand for generations to come as one of the finest exemplars of first-rate social fiction in the United States.

# CHAPTER ONE

## THE WORLD OF *RABBIT AT REST*

Everything has some tiny reason, even when we can't see it.

—John Updike, *Rabbit at Rest*

As with the first three novels of the Rabbit tetralogy, *Rabbit at Rest* starts with a precise statement of year, month, week, day, and place. Ten years after Rabbit had been declared a hostage of fortune, we find him at the airport in Miami with his wife Janice. They are on their way to pick up their son Nelson, their daughter-in-law Pru, and their two grandchildren, Roy (four years old) and Judy (almost nine years old), who are flying in for a five-day visit. The year, we easily infer, is 1988, the month is December, the week is the last of the month, and it is the Tuesday after Christmas of "the last year of Reagan's reign"(6). To be more precise, it is December 27, 1988.

Virtually every incident of the story may be set precisely in time and space so that not only may we say with certainty, for instance, that the first chapter starts on December 27[1] and ends on December 31, 1988, but we may also categorically affirm that (1) on December 28 Rabbit plays golf with his Jewish friends; (2) on December 29 he and Janice take their two grandchildren on a tour of Thomas Alva Edison's winter home and the Sarasota Jungle Gardens, after which they watch the movie *Working Girl*; (3) on December 30 Rabbit, his daughter-in-law, and her two children spend the morning at the Omni Bayview where Rabbit suffers a heart attack (we also know that the telephone rings in their apartment at precisely 12:25 P.M. to inform his wife that he has been taken to the hospital); and (4) on December 31 Nelson, Pru, and the grandchildren fly back to Pennsylvania.

The same obsessive precision may be found in every chapter and most of the thirty-five subchapters of the novel[2] so that step by step the reader is invited to read history into story and story into history, perceiving with little effort that one cannot exist without the other and that the characters are not only *in* history but *with* history, being energized by it, moved by it, and justified by it. In other words, Updike's characters are not only interpreters and proprietors of history but are also interpreted and owned by it.

For the last five years, Rabbit and Janice have spent half the year in Florida. This way they have avoided the harsh northern winters and, conveniently, conflicts with Nelson, who now runs their Toyota dealership. Because of this peculiarity, the novel is

---

[1] In his introduction to *Harry Angstrom* Updike mistakenly states that *Rabbit at Rest* begins on December 28, 1988. Since December 28, 1988, was a Wednesday, not a Tuesday, December 27 is the correct date.

[2] Chapter 2 starts around April 10, 1989, and ends precisely on May 10, 1989. Chapter 3 starts on June 19, 1989, and ends on September 22, 1989. With little effort, the same precision can be established for the subchapters. We know, for example, that Rabbit starts driving south on Thursday, August 31, 1989. When he enters his car, the digital clock shows that it is 10:07 P.M. For a complete chronology of the novel see Appendix 1.

organized into three chapters: the first taking place in Florida, the second in Pennsylvania, and the third in an in-between state which belongs more to the body and mind than to the world of geography. It is a state called MI (for myocardiac infarction) to which Rabbit has been traveling with suicidal determination. He has become indolent and a compulsive eater of unhealthy food. And, as the epigraph to the novel reminds us, "food to the indolent is poison."

Rabbit is now fifty-five years old—an age which he feels has enwrapped him "like a set of blankets the decades have brought one by one" (6). He weighs two hundred thirty pounds "the kindest scales say" (6), and as his always empathetic narrator puts it, he is "ready to succumb to the heaviness of being" (76). The blankets of the decades and the number of pounds trouble his body and soul. He has a serious heart problem, and as time passes, he becomes more and more aware of "his wasting muscles and accumulating fat" (78). To his surprise, he observes that things not even as old as himself are being sold as antiques. Everything seems to point towards the inexorability of his approaching death.

And death, in both the narrow and broad senses of the word, is doubtless the major theme of *Rabbit at Rest*. As Mathew Wilson points out, the novel is concerned with death from the first to the last sentence. One could argue that death has always been a theme in the Rabbit novels. Hadn't Rabbit been called Mr. Death in 1959? Isn't the death of his baby daughter in *Rabbit, Run* a major theme? In *Rabbit Redux* we have the tragic death of Jill, and in *Rabbit Is Rich* Rabbit is indeed rich, among other things, because of the death of his father-in-law. Although Rabbit has become rich, he also is aware that he is now a grandfather—a fearful intimation that his newborn granddaughter is just "another nail in his coffin" (*RA* 1045). Death has always been present as a motivating force in Rabbit's life, but this is the first time both the pos-

sibility and probability of imminent death point towards him. As
Sanford Pinsker puts it, "Updike's protagonist becomes another
mirror held up to America: its excesses, its exhaustion, and most
of all, its fear of death" (735). For Rabbit death has become something very near and clear, although his older friends in Miami and
the national longevity statistics could easily show him that natural death might be postponed for at least two more decades.[3]
Medical knowledge and some personal attention to diet and exercise—all of which Rabbit feels a suicidal urge to disobey—could
also postpone his death, even *after* his serious heart attacks.

But the obsession with death has less to do with the idea of its
certainty at one point or another in Rabbit's life than with the
scene in which he is placed. In *Rabbit at Rest* the notion of death
acquires a special significance because of the ubiquitous presence
of time and place referents and all that goes with them—
incidents, events, circumstances, and locations. These referents, it
appears, were all selected by a historically situated narrator who
picked them out of a world of almost infinite possibilities in order
to make his story and characters tick.

In this context, therefore, death acquires an emblematic and
metaphoric meaning. Not only is Rabbit's death more than his
own, but it is also associated with middle America's perception
that it is losing control over the new forces which have become
manifest in the country: international terrorism, the end of the
Cold War, foreign debt, foreign domination, feminism, AIDS,
drug addiction, and others.

---

[3] The National Institute on Aging revealed on June 12, 1989, the day President
George Bush turned sixty-five, that the average life expectancy for Americans at
birth was 71.7 years for men and 78.3 years for women. For someone like Bush,
who has already reached sixty-five, life expectancy is 80 years for men and 83.9
years for women.

The causes of death are clearly more than physical illness. They have to do especially with the national collective behavior which, with every decade that passes, becomes more foreign and unacceptable to a mind like Rabbit's. His present values were forged in the fifties and since then have been submitted to the implacable forces of a changing scene. As I argued in *Updike's America,* "Updike's need to place his novels so precisely in time and space expresses the conviction that his character, in his middleness, can only become maladapted and tensional if scene dislocations are promoted. Harry's conservative and adaptive tendencies would make him live in almost ape-like harmony with his environment had it not been made into a constantly changing element" (9). The time has come again when adaptations need to be made to redefine middleness and make survival possible. For Rabbit this is not an easy task, and his difficulties in *Rabbit at Rest* start with the place and time in which he finds himself when we meet him.

That Florida as a location is important for enhancing Rabbit's state of mind can be seen from the beginning of the novel. Here at "his home away from home"(73) everything seems to be associated with old people. He sees "decrepit bodies" (30), "busloads of old retired people" (93), and "cars being driven by old people so shrunken they can hardly see over the hood" (106). Not only are his friends older than he and Janice but the whole structure and organization of the city and state seem to have mainly the elderly in mind. The airport terminal itself is "a long low white building like a bigger version of the sunstruck clinics—dental, chiropractic, arthritic, cardiac, legal, legal-medical—that line the boulevards of this state dedicated to the old. You park at a lot only a few steps away from the door of sliding brown glass: the whole state babies you" (4).

Although Florida is regarded by his friends as the best state for a permanent vacation, Rabbit's mind is set less on fun and more on thinking and worrying about the visible and undeniable fact that he and Janice, too, are growing old. They are not like Nelson and Pru; they are not like young couples who still "give off this heat" (101). Instead, like all the old people around them, they "give off the musty smell of dead flower stalks, rotting in the vase" (101). Even Dr. Morris, with whom Rabbit has his last appointment in Miami, "gives off an old man's sad leathery, moldy smell" (474)—a smell that more and more he identifies on himself. Months after having left Florida, Rabbit drives around Brewer and tries to reenergize himself with the life of the young on the street—"these lives that are young and rising like sap where his is old and sinking" (186). Wherever he goes, especially in Miami, Rabbit is aware of the inexorable process of aging, decay, and death.

Yet, from the world of Florida—where "just not being senile is considered great" (113), where music becomes nothing but a noise to make us forget the eternal silence of death (4), and where, as Nelson puts it, "all you can deal for . . . is Geritol" (161)—to the world at large, things do not seem to change very much. At the airport, as Rabbit runs his eyes over the news in the newspapers, "a sense of doom regrows its claws around his heart" (8). The newspapers, too, are full of death.

As in the previous novels, Rabbit is always watching the news, trying to see if he finds a hidden meaning in it, something significant for his life. In the process he appropriates the news and brings it into his life, so that the news itself, as a textured scene, becomes a way of understanding the workings of his mind and, as a consequence, the inner conflicts of his soul.

The historical scene in which Rabbit operates is present on virtually every page of the novel. From a purely quantitative perspective, one could be misled to argue that history is merely background. Were we, however, for simplification purposes, to

reduce the scene to the names of persons, we might easily conclude that the spectrum covered is so broad that we would have
to deal with personalities of regional, national, and international
recognition on every other page, encompassing concerns that vary
from popular music to religion, to movies, to television, to politics
at all levels, to economics, to sports, etc. Names such as Rock
Hudson, Donald Trump, Michael Dukakis, George Bush, Ronald
Reagan, Ollie North, Mikhail Gorbachev, Melanie Griffith, Johnny
Carson, Manuel Antonio Noriega, Ayatollah Khomeini, Hirohito,
Dalai Lama, Pope John Paul II, Jim Bakker, Louis W. Sullivan,
Ivan Boeski, Edward I. Koch, David N. Dinkins, Frank Sinatra,
Marlon Brando, Helmut Kohl, and so on, are scattered throughout
the novel as knots which tie together the complexity of the scene
in which the characters of the novel are immersed.

The scene is, however, construed by much more than just lists
of names. As Updike himself points out in his 1968 interview with
Charles Thomas Samuels, "My fiction about the daily doings of
ordinary people has more history in it than history books, just as
there is more breathing history in archeology than in a list of declared wars and changes of government" (Plath 37). A list is then
merely a point of reference unable to generate "breathing history," unable to unveil a life or a living scene, unless it is made,
through various interconnections, into an active part of a network
of relations. What makes the scene come to life is the generative
power its texturized constituents have over the story.

It is true that not all of the names, events, and circumstances
have the same generative power in the story. It is a mistake, however, to conceive of history in the Rabbit novels as mere background. History is to such an extent an integral and interconnected part of the story that it would be no exaggeration to say
that without history there would be no story, or at least no story
worth reading. It is not as though when taking away the frame

there would still be the picture to behold. The truth is that without history there is no picture, for Updike's text as much as Rabbit's mind is nourished by the historical scene.

Are the Rabbit novels sustained by *any* of the elements of the historical scene? Clearly not. There is abundant evidence to indicate that Rabbit's exposure is basically to a scene which has been texturized for him by the country's hegemonic forces. The Portuguese poet Fernando Pessoa once wrote, "The universe is not my idea; my idea of the universe is my idea." With Rabbit things are slightly different, for neither can we say that the world is Rabbit's idea nor that his idea of the world is his idea. His ideological other-directedness is evident at every step of his trajectory. His life is especially nourished by those events, persons, incidents, and circumstances which enhance the ideological frame that has historically been construed for him, namely nationalism, racism, sexism, anticommunism, individualism, and religiosity. The scenic forces that support this ideological frame have greater generative power and are, thus, of greater importance to the story.

What are some of these major events or clearly historical circumstances that populate Rabbit's world in *Rabbit at Rest* during the last year of Reagan's presidency and the first year of Bush's? Although there may be (and perhaps should be) disagreement on this question given the possible imprints produced by reader participation, it is reasonable to suggest at least six major historical scenic components generating action in the story: (1) the various airplane accidents: a) the midair explosion of a PanAmerican Boeing 747 on December 21, 1988, over Lockerbie, Scotland; b) the explosion on a jet flying from Atlanta to Rochester on December 27, 1988; c) the DC-10 jet crash at Sioux City, Iowa, on July 19, 1989; d) the USAir plane crash in the Hudson River Bay, in New

York; e) the crash of a French DC-10;[1] (2) the end of the Cold War; (3) the foreign debt crisis and the Japanese economic invasion; (4) the AIDS epidemic; (5) the war on drugs; and (6) abortion and feminism.

Each of these issues incorporates within itself a number of other precisely placed historical events, most of which fall under one or the other of the above categories and all of which acquire importance because of the ideological charge which Rabbit imprints upon them or retrieves from them. Following is a discussion on how each of these major themes, dramatized through the energy of specific historic events, contributes to the writing of Rabbit's story in *Rabbit at Rest*.

---

[1] An explosion aboard a PanAmerican Airways Boeing 747 killed all two hundred fifty-nine persons aboard and eleven on the ground when it fell on the village of Lockerbie, Scotland. British officials said on February 16, 1989, that a bomb had been hidden in a radio-cassette player and had probably been put aboard at Frankfurt, West Germany, where the flight originated (Garruth 820).

On December 27, 1988, an Eastern Airlines Boeing 727 landed safely in Atlanta after its fuselage ruptured in midair. None of the one hundred ten people on board was seriously injured.

A United Airlines DC-10 jet crashed short of the runway at Sioux City, Iowa [on July 19, 1989], and one hundred and twelve of the two hundred and ninety-six persons aboard died. The pilot had struggled for forty-five minutes to control the plane after an explosion in its tail engine. On November 1, 1990, the National Transportation Safety Board blamed the airline for failure to detect the flaw in the engine that caused it to disintegrate (Garruth 820).

On September 21, 1989, a USAir jetliner plunged into the Bay off La Guardia airport in New York. Three people were reported killed and fifty-one injured.

The French DC-10 disappeared on a flight from Chad to France on September 19, 1989. Apparently it exploded in midair, the explosion being caused by a bomb. One hundred seventy-one people were on board.

# CHAPTER TWO

## THE PLANE OF DEATH

Unlike most writers, I believe that there is a connection between political events and the life of a common working man.

—John Updike, *Conversations*

References to plane crashes are spread throughout the five hundred-plus pages of *Rabbit at Rest,* with Rabbit repeating almost verbatim, months later, what he observed on December 27, 1988, at the time the story begins, namely that there have been "a lot of disasters lately" (233). In other words, Rabbit is not sporadically but constantly reminded of the terror and death that accompany these crashes. It is this terror and death which he appropriates and makes his own.

Early in the novel Rabbit recalls the deaths of rock singer Roy Orbison, of ABC's African American anchorman Max Robinson, and "then before Christmas that PanAm flight 103, ripping open like a rotten melon five miles above Scotland and dropping all these bodies and flaming wreckage all over the golf course and the streets of this little town like Glockamorra, what was its real name, Lockerbie" (8).[1] The accident with PanAm flight 103 happened on December 21 and was in all the papers on December 22. Rabbit, like most Americans, carries with him six days of bombardment with frequent news on the accident, knowing by now all the details—flight number, kind of airplane, age of airplane, height the airplane was flying, the name of the town, probable causes of the explosion, the reports of eyewitnesses, etc.

As it must have happened with all those who read, saw, and heard the news, Rabbit uses the details as the basis for images or fictions of his own: the plane bursts open "like a rotten melon," the bodies dropping over Scotland "like wet melon seeds" (10). He imagines the terror of it all. He imagines what it must have been like:

> Sitting there in your seat being lulled by the hum of the big Rolls-Royce engines and the stewardesses bringing the clinking drinks caddy and the feeling of having caught the plane and nothing to do now but relax and then with a roar and giant ripping noise and scattered screams this whole cozy world dropping away and nothing under you but black space and your chest squeezed by the terrible unbreathable cold. (8)

He thinks of Lockerbie as Glockamorra, an allusion to Sodom and Gomorra—the cities punished by God for their sins. But even the possibility of this interpretation of deserved punishment cannot erase the terror from his mind. As he appropriates the historical moment, making the axis of history read directly into the axis of the story, he recalls the death of his baby daughter, Rebecca June, who drowned thirty years earlier. Rabbit still cannot accept what happened then. Had God pulled the plug in

---

[1] Roy Orbison, well-known for singing "Pretty Woman," was born in 1936 and died in 1988. Max Robinson died (reportedly of AIDS) on December 20, 1988, a week before the novel begins.

the bathtub and let the water run out, the baby would not have died. But God Almighty, "who set the stars in place" (10), for some mysterious reason did not do it: "It would have been so easy for him . . . to have it unhappen. Or to delete from the universe whatever it was that exploded that PanAm 747 over Scotland" (10). One cannot help observing that here Rabbit's God closely resembles the all-American cinema-produced Superman.

Rabbit wonders how much the passengers and the crew members knew about what was happening to them as they fell through the dark and the cold, "their hearts pumping," still alive. His concern is not that of the cold, analytically-minded airline personnel. To the airline, as Rabbit sees it, people mean nothing but flashes on a radar screen: "A blip on the screen, then no blip on the screen, who cares?" (10).

To his astonishment, for him, too, the horror of the PanAm accident gradually begins to dissipate into the routine of just another television show.[2] As he watches an airplane landing at the Miami airport, "he imagines the plane exploding as it touches down, ignited by one of its glints, in a ball of red flame shadowed in black *like you see on TV all the time*, and he is shocked to find within himself, imagining this, not much emotion, just a cold thrill at being a witness" (10, my emphasis).

But Rabbit does care, and he reacts very strongly to his own fictionalizing of the accident. As he sees it, for his granddaughter Judy it is like just another movie. For children these things only happen to other people, he thinks, but he is old enough to realize it may happen to anybody, himself included. Every moment of his life seems to be affected by the accident; his mind, having been bombarded by the news of the day which claimed that specialists

---

[2] For an interesting discussion of this television-cultivated detachment, see Stacey Olster's "Rabbit Rerun: Updike's Replay of Popular Culture in *Rabbit at Rest*," *Modern Fiction Studies* 37, no. 1 (1991): 45–59.

determined that traces of explosives had been found in a leather suitcase, creates its own metaphors.[3] His wife Janice, as a consequence, no longer carries a simple pocketbook with her, but instead she carries "a black leather pocketbook packed like a bomb, the old-fashioned round kind people used to throw and not the flattened Semtex that terrorists smuggle into suitcases in airplanes" (282). The international event, with all its gruesome details, has become part of Rabbit's brooding about daily life.

While playing golf with his Jewish friends on December 28, Rabbit cannot avoid mentioning the accident. To his surprise and disappointment, he discovers that for them the event is merely a technical and political matter. Technically it is, as for Judy, a bomb: "it was a bomb, silly," his granddaughter tells him, "it had to be" (79). Politically, his friends see it as part of a larger issue— the Arab-Israeli conflict—a conflict that they perceive to be affecting their lives more directly. Rabbit had not meant his question as technical or political; they miss his meaning:

> "I mean," he says, "how the hell do you think it feels? Sitting there and having the plane explode?"
> "Well, I bet it wakes you up," Ed says.
> "They didn't feel a thing," Bernie says considerately, sensing Harry's personal worry. "Zero. It was over that quick." (69)

It is interesting to note that on December 22, 1988, the *New York Times* reported that aviation authorities believed, since the plane disappeared from radar screens without an emergency call from the cockpit, whatever it was that brought it down must have happened instantaneously.

---

[3] On December 26, the CBS *Evening News* reported that investigators claimed to have found evidence proving that a "bomb caused the PanAm plane crash. British investigators reported finding a suitcase and debris that appear to have been damaged by a bomb."

Their discussion, however, abandons these technicalities as quickly as it falls back into the political realm and then fades again into golf. Quite obviously, for Rabbit the meaning of the event is not merely technical or political. It is beyond all that; it has superseded these realms. He has appropriated an emotional, spiritual, religious dimension that he identifies in the event and which forbids the technical and the political to manifest themselves, for these will only lead to more analysis and are incapable of showing him the meaning of life and the rules which govern it. He can hardly read about it in the papers any longer. He cannot overcome the horror of "everything upside-down and void of mercy and meaning" (91). Thus the horror and terror of the passengers, victims of a world which makes no sense, become his own. In his empathy, he metaphorically boards their plane and shares their suffering and fate:

Up, up; the air thins, the barometer registers, the timer begins to tick[4] as the plane snugly bores through darkness . . . The image, like a seed at last breaking its shell in moist soil, awakens in Harry the realization that even now as he lies in this antiseptic white fog tangled in tubes and ties of blood and marriage he is just like the people he felt sorry for, falling from the burst-open airplane: he too is falling, helplessly falling, toward death. What met them was no more than what awaits him. Reality broke upon those passengers . . . and that same icy black reality has broken upon him; death is not a domesticated pet of life but a beast that swallowed baby Amber and baby Becky and *all those Syracuse students*[5] and returning soldiers, and will swallow him, it is truly there under him,

---

[4] On December 29, 1988, the *New York Times* reported that "the device used to destroy the PanAmerican . . . jet was almost certainly set off by an altimeter or the bellows mechanism from an aneroid barometer . . . an attacker would want to make sure that the bomb would explode in flight and not on the ground. For this, a simple timing device would not suffice, since a departure delay would lead to a premature blast."

vast as a planet at night, gigantic and totally his. His death . . . he feels all
but suffocated by the terror." (176, my emphasis)

It takes some knowledge of what the media were writing and
saying to appreciate how much Updike's text grows out of the
heat of history. When his son Nelson tells Rabbit that "they think
they know exactly what kind of bomb it was—there's a kind with
a barometric device that activates a timer when a certain altitude
is reached" (176), Nelson is repeating almost verbatim the *New
York Times* and other major national newspapers. Nelson, like his
father and the other characters in the novel, has also been
historicized.

As a further curiosity, it may be important to register that on
December 31, 1988, which is the precise date Nelson brings Harry
the newspaper, the *New York Times* reported that the bomb was
probably prepared with two barometric detonators, not just one.
This would cause the pressure to first activate a timing device,
then later the bomb itself. This could explain why the plane
would have time to gain height and snugly "bore through
darkness" before actually exploding. Reports say that the
explosion occurred fifty-two minutes after takeoff. Animations
demonstrating how the device was triggered were run on ABC's
*World News Tonight* on December 30.

Although Rabbit relives his daughter's drowning once more
and although he identifies completely with the passengers of the
plane, he also ends up "politicizing" the issue and blames "those
damn Arabs" (176) for the accident. In fact, by December 31 it had
already been established that a bomb had caused the explosion.
On December 30 Sheila Rule had already reported for the *New
York Times* that "an unidentified caller claiming to represent a

---

[5] The *New York Times* of December 22, 1988, carries this front-page headline:
"Jetliner Carrying 258 to US Crashes in Scottish Town—All Believed Dead." The

pro-Iranian group . . . took responsibility for the PanAm bombing." The unidentified man was said to have a foreign accent and claimed to represent the "Guardians of the Islamic Revolution, a pro-Iranian group." The man made it very clear that unless America stopped protecting twenty-eight-year-old Riza Pahlevi, son of the late Shah of Iran, the new year would also feature "another present from us." Similar reports could be seen the same day on ABC and CBS evening news, with reference made to various well-known Palestinian terrorists. Rabbit's confusing Iranians with Arabs, therefore, should not surprise us. It is also the confusion shared by his two Jewish friends earlier in the novel, and to a large extent the confusion of the media in general. In the context of the Arab-Israeli conflict, as in the context of the novel, the confusion (because of Iran's historic anti-Israel stand and because of America's historic pro-Israel stand) is probably deliberate. Rabbit's judgment, however, seems to be more the result of an appropriated national ideological stance than the result of political analysis and inference.

Talking with Charlie Stavros about the PanAm crash and other airplane disasters does not seem to help much either. With his metonymical approach to life, Charlie tries to make Rabbit see that, although the number of accidents seems large, it is really statistically insignificant considering how crowded the world has become with its five billion inhabitants. His view that "there's a crush on, and it's not going to get any better" (233) makes Rabbit feel that he himself is one of too many inhabitants this world has. Again the thought of death is inevitable, for with all this overcrowding, statistics seem to prove, "when you die you do the world a favor" (233).

The PanAm accident did not, however, affect only Rabbit and the characters in the novel. The novel tells us that it also affected

---

subhead says: "Syracuse University had 36 people aboard."

the security at the JFK airport. On August 31, 1989, "a new bomb detector, called a TNA, for thermal neutron analysis" was installed (439). Strangely enough, despite the Federal Aviation Administration's announcement that this machine could detect even bombs like the one that destroyed the PanAmerican airplane over Scotland, Rabbit believes that the new device would not have saved those people's lives. Historicizing Rabbit's doubt throws some light on his belief. The explanation is that Rabbit has also read the experts' comments that the machine can be fooled by other substances that contain small amounts of nitrogen, like clothing, leather, wool, or cheese. The conclusion is that *they* would not have been saved and that, by implication, neither would he.[6]

Near the end of the novel, although Rabbit cannot fail to notice the large number of accidents occurring, he seems to be less concerned about them, as if all the rest are anticlimactic after the explosion of the PanAmerican airplane—just another boring television show: "Like everything else on the news, you get bored, it gets to seem a gimmick, like all those TV time-outs in football" (501). Yet it would be a mistake to assume that Rabbit has become bored with the news of the accidents. What is at stake here are the forces of his ideological makeup. Rabbit's nationalism naturally leads him to view an attack by foreign terrorists as targeted at the heart of America—his heart. But an attack by the same foreign terrorists who shot down in the name of Allah a French airplane with one hundred seventy-one people aboard he doesn't mind that much, not as much as the Lockerbie PanAm bomb.

---

[6]Airliners were ordered by the government to install a thermal neutron analyzer, a new bomb detecting device, at all major airports in the country on August 30, 1989. The Federal Aviation Administration claimed that the device could detect all types of bombs, including plastic explosives like the one that destroyed PanAm flight 103.

Rabbit's declaration of boredom, however, is not apolitical, as one might be led to believe. His nationalism has grown beyond politics—it has become a religious faith. It has placed the rest of the world into otherness, restricting the extension of his sympathies. He will acknowledge that one hundred seventy-one persons were killed, but somehow it means less, it means little, it means next to nothing, for they were not Americans. Rabbit's nationalism impedes his identification with humanity to express itself and as a consequence inhibits the creation of metaphors expressing his sympathy with the passengers' suffering. In this case, borrowing Rabbit's own metaphor, he was not on the plane. This would also explain why the shooting down of a civilian Iranian jet by the American *Vincennes*, although mentioned in the text, does not occupy Rabbit's mind (456).[7] Along the same line of reasoning, one wonders why the accident with a Cuban airplane which crashed on September 4, 1989 (during the chronological time of the novel), has been completely neglected. The answer seems to be that the ideologically-oriented historical preferences arc not only Rabbit's—they are also Updike's, who needs these preferences to portray middleness. In other words, it is not that Rabbit forgets about these and other events—it is the novel's texturized scene which denies him the right to know about them and to remember them. It takes the memory of a history-minded reader to uncover the fact that the Cuban airplane accident barely made the news and that the forgetfulness of the historical scene matches that of the novel. It is as much a strategic forgetfulness for America as it is for Rabbit.

---

[7] A United States Navy warship downed a civilian Iranian airliner in the Persian Gulf on July 4, 1988, killing all two hundred ninety persons on board. The airliner was said to have been mistaken for an F-14.

# CHAPTER THREE

## THE DEATH OF AN ERA

Without the cold war, what's the point of being an American?

—John Updike, *Rabbit at Rest*

At the same time terrorist bombs planted by foreigners are causing the deaths of many Americans, the Cold War is coming to an end, the use of drugs is rampant, AIDS is taking its toll, and abortion and feminism are causing divisiveness and instability. All of these forces challenge old ways, beliefs, and assumptions and constantly interfere with Rabbit's life. We cannot imagine him in the eighties without these forces in the same way that we cannot conceive of him in the fifties without the Korean War, the highways, television, and the Dalai Lama; or in the sixties without hippies, the Civil Rights movement, the Vietnam War, and the moon landing; or in the seventies without the Iranian hostage crisis, the energy crisis, the long lines at gas stations, the Toyota invasion, and President Carter's crisis of confidence.

As he did in previous decades, Rabbit rehearses resistance to these forces, for they promote change and produce fear. In the eighties he is aware that he was brought up in "a world where war was not strange but change was: the world stood still so you could grow up in it" (461). To a large extent then Rabbit's struggle can be said to be motivated by resentment—resentment brought about by a society which refuses to allow itself to be pinned down, understood, and controlled. Change is the driving force, both of society and of Rabbit's resentment, and that explains why his pain will not pass:

> Resentment churns within him. He resents Nelson's getting all this attention for being a prodigal son. He resents Janice's learning new words and pushing outward into new fields, away from him. He resents the fact that the world is so full of debt and nobody to pay—not Mexico or Brazil, not the sleazy S and L banks, not Nelson. Rabbit never had much use for old-fashioned ethics but their dissolution eats at his bones. (400)

For Rabbit, things just aren't the same any more, and this is especially noticeable in the younger generations, with whom he no longer shares the "same songs, attitudes toward wars, the same rules and radio shows" (402). He can no longer "gauge the possibilities and impossibilities" (402). Their references are not his. He seems to belong to another era altogether.

It is interesting to note that in the eighties Rabbit places the beginning of his crisis in the fifties, when he believes his world started to change, making adaptation a necessary condition for survival. In his view, it started when "the system . . . decided to close Kroll's down, just because shoppers had stopped coming in because downtown had become frightening to white people" (461). For him Kroll's department store was "bigger than a church, older than a courthouse" (461). With the laws of God and the laws of man being transferred from the place, the world began to lose its stability, familiarity, and predictability. Instead, it became transitory, temporary, a prey to monetary interests. For Rabbit the closing down of Kroll's had a meaning which transcended the mere demise of a particular business enterprise. It meant also the probable end of the old social order and of all its institutions—commercial, legal, financial, religious—leading to a world of anomie: "If Kroll's could go, the courthouse could go, the banks could go . . . they could close down God himself" (461).

As the old worlds erode and are pushed to a crisis at every decade's end, Rabbit continues his struggle for adaptation. His America has been threatened by blacks, hippies, Soviets, communists in general, Arabs, Japanese—foreigners of all nationalities—and now in the eighties, after a decade of Reaganism and of "nobody minding the store, making money out of nothing running up debt, trusting in God" (9), he realizes that although some old enemies are no longer there, new ones, more ominous and cruel, again threaten his world.

Now that the Cold War is over Rabbit thinks that America has lost a major part of its identity. He asks himself, "Without the cold war, what's the point of being an American?" (442). The question is not one to be lightly dismissed; it becomes extremely meaningful when we consider that Rabbit is somebody who has had anticommunism as a major goal in life ("if you don't want it, the Commies do" [*RRE* 152]) and who, along with Reagan, pushed the world toward a new Cold War throughout the eighties.[1] For him, the end of the Cold War is less a goal achieved than it is the loss of purpose in life: "[The Cold War] gave you a reason to get up in the morning" (353).

What is to be done now that the goal has been taken away? This "bizarre nostalgia for the Cold War," as Peter Tarnoff calls it, is not only Rabbit's. Tarnoff complains that, strangely enough, the

[1] For an interesting discussion of the topic see Noam Chomsky's *Toward a New Cold War*. New York: Pantheon Books, 1982.

top Bush administration officials seemed to let pass the idea that the Cold War was not such a bad thing after all and that its end might be harmful to American interests, especially in Europe, now that world power relations are no longer clearly defined and new countries are participating in international disputes. The power which was once concentrated in Washington and Moscow has now been diffused among a large number of states, forcing the administration to define a new agenda with a multitude of low-profile engagements.

But perhaps the most remarkable example of this bizarre nostalgia is Francis Fukuyama's understanding that the end of the East-West conflict is also the end of history. The triumph of the democratic and liberal models of social organization over the authoritarian forms of fascism and communism represents for him the end of humanity's ideological evolution and is no reason for joy:

> The end of history will be a very sad time . . . the struggle for recognition, the willingness to risk one's life for a purely abstract goal, the worldwide ideological struggle that called forth daring, courage, imagination and idealism will be replaced by economic calculation, the endless solving of technical problems, environmental concerns . . . I can feel in myself, and see in others around me, a powerful nostalgia for the time when history existed. Perhaps this very prospect of boredom at the end of history will serve to get history started once again. (18)

Rabbit seems to have appropriated this Fukuyaman spirit in full. Not only has he lost his goal of giving his life if necessary in the fight against communists, but he also, like Fukuyama, associates the new era with the afterlife and the endless bickering about economic and technological issues. "The thing about the afterlife," he thinks, "[is that] it kept this life within bounds somehow, like the Russians. Now there's just Japan, and technology, and the profit motive, and getting all you can while you can" (272). For Rabbit, too, the end of the Cold War looks like the end of history.

As with the anticommunist ideology of the fifties, Rabbit's time is done. The communists are "acting confused," voted out by the people in Poland, denounced by Gorbachev as crooks in the Soviet Union, at risk in China. Rabbit cannot help asking: "Who ever would have thought we'd live to see the day?" (353). Yet, it is true that the Chinese communists and the Nicaraguan communists and a few others are still around and deserve his attention. This is precisely why Rabbit follows with great interest the developments in eastern Europe and China. The events in China, with throngs of students protesting the communist regime, fighting for freedom, and (according to Rabbit) wanting to be like Americans, are present throughout the novel. And since the novel's chronology matches perfectly the chronology of the corresponding historical events, it is interesting to notice that Rabbit's concern over China and eastern Europe coincides with that of the newspapers. China and Poland gain increased attention in the media and in the novel the more the Moscow-Washington talks seem to show promising results, suggesting that perhaps the emphasis on these two countries was the Establishment's way of cushioning middle America's landing in the post–Cold War era. The novel's presentation of the crackdown on the pro-democracy protesters on June 4, 1989, when thousands of troops retook Tiananmen Square, firing on unarmed civilians and killing about five hundred of them, shows that Rabbit also sees China as "the other side." For him the crackdown is not surprising. What surprises him is that for a month "kids were allowed to run the show and nobody knew what to do about it! It's like nobody's in charge of the other side any more" (353). In a way he seems to condone the Chinese government's determination to reaffirm its authority through violence. The end of the war with the Soviets requires that he find a "reason to get up in the morning." It demands a new enemy, and the Chinese may well become that enemy as long as they stick to their ironhanded totalitarianism and keep communism alive. Updike's latest novel, *Toward the End of Time* (1997), in which he imagines America in the year 2020 after a devastating war with China, seems to indicate that Rabbit's concerns are not only his but also his creator's.

"Reagan's reign" thus represented a fertile soil for Rabbit's ideology to flourish. Reagan's "America is standing tall again" policy and his belligerent anti-Soviet, anticommunist, anti-Arab stance made Carter's crisis of confidence a thing of the past.[2]

Reagan successfully managed to restore nationalism and national pride despite the obvious disasters on the military, social, and economic fronts. As Reagan left the presidency with the highest overall approval ratings of any president in the history of American poll-taking (68 percent), he felt authorized to name the "recovery of our morale" as one of the two things of which he was very proud: "America is respected again in the world and looked to for leadership" (*HD* 18). Indeed, a *New York Times*/CBS poll indicates that at the end of Reagan's second term, 38 percent of Americans said they trusted the government "most of the time"— a significant 16 percent increase when compared to the last year of Jimmy Carter's presidency.

The second thing Reagan claimed to be proud of was the economic recovery. He mentioned the nineteen million new jobs created; the change in attitude of the industrialized nations

---

[2] On April 27, 1983, Reagan declared during a joint session of Congress that "the national security of all Americans is at stake in Central America. If we cannot defend ourselves there, we cannot expect to prevail elsewhere. Our credibility would collapse, our alliances would crumble, and the safety of our homeland would be put at jeopardy." Two years later, in his State of the Union address, he vowed to aid anticommunist "freedom fighters" everywhere in the world.

toward the United States asking him to "tell [them] about the American miracle"; and his tax reduction and deregulation plans, which he claimed led to "the longest peacetime expansion in our history: real family income up, the poverty rate down, entrepreneurship booming, an explosion in research and new technology" (*HD* 19). Most of this information was not only questioned by historians, critics, and political adversaries but declared false by statistical evidence. Not only had national and foreign debt increased significantly but education had deteriorated, poverty had worsened, and crime and drug use were on the rise. Even the standards of ethics in government were perceived as declining by 33 percent of the people (probably the result of the Iran-contra scandal). Only 8 percent claimed there had been improvement in this area.

Yet while the harshest critics identified Reagan with "the worst abuses we've ever seen of public trust and the environment in the history of the presidency" and with "the worst civil rights record of any administration in several decades" (Gimlin 17), Rabbit, in perfect accordance with the polls that showed a 72 percent approval rating among white males, approved of Reagan's administration.[3] He does have some ambiguous feelings about "the Great Communicator," as Reagan came to be known, but overall he has to admit that he liked him:

> He liked Reagan. He liked the foggy voice, the smile, the big shoulders, the way he kept his head wagging during the long pauses, the way he floated above facts, knowing there was more to government than facts, and the way he could change direction while saying he was going straight ahead, pulling out of Beirut, getting cozy with Gorby, running up national debt. The strange thing was, except for the hopeless down-and-outers, the world became a better place under him. The communists fell

---

[3] The same polls showed that only 40 percent of African Americans approved of Reagan's administration.

apart, except for in Nicaragua, and even there he put them on the defensive. The guy had a magic touch. He was a dream man. Harry dares say, "under Reagan, you know, it was like Anesthesia." (62)

Reagan's "magic touch," however, seems to have come less from his foggy voice, monarchic statesman's posture, and long pauses than from his identification with living and widespread Cold War values. His magic touch is in fact an inextricable part of the new Cold War which characterized his presidency and which can be especially perceived in Reagan's attempt to characterize the Soviet Union as the empire of evil.[4] The sense of America being "pushed around" by Iran, Nicaragua, the Arabs, and others, so noticeable during the Carter era, had disappeared under Reagan, so that "pulling out of Beirut,"[5] instead of being regarded as a political defeat, was actually and quickly perceived by middle America as victory, transformed as it was into another anticommunist military action—the invasion of Grenada.

The speed with which Reagan managed to divert the attention of the media is astonishing, in retrospect—so much so that the impression is that the casualties of Beirut are actually the toll to be paid for victory over the communists in the tiny island of

---

[4] The downing of a Korean civilian jet by the Soviets on September 1, 1983, was perhaps the highest point of Reagan's successful media campaign to make communism and evil synonymous. By September 14 Reagan declared that he considered the "Soviet regime a dictatorship with no regard for human values or rights" (TNIA 1855). No other piece of news gained as much attention throughout the decade, with over one hundred twenty national network broadcast entries, some occupying as much as 90 percent of the news broadcasts. The Soviet Union argued that the Korean plane was flying over its airspace and that, despite warnings, it refused to change course. The Soviets argued that the plane was on a spy mission and cited as evidence the fact that other American aircraft were listening in on the radio conversation. Not until December 13 was the pilot's error recognized by the International Civil Aviation Organization.

[5] The bombing of the marine headquarters in Beirut occurred on October 23, 1983, killing two hundred forty-one marines.

Grenada. Rabbit carries the Beirut experience with him as something not fully explained and attributes Reagan's getting away with it to his magic touch. Had he connected Beirut to Grenada his interpretation might have been different, but this understanding is strategically denied him by Updike and requires a reader's memory to be made possible as a new perspective. It should be recalled that the invasion of Grenada occurred only two days after the bombing of the marine headquarters in Beirut.

It must be pointed out that in *Rabbit at Rest* we meet Rabbit at the end of one presidency and the beginning of another. "Reagan's reign" is coming to an end, and Bush is about to be inaugurated. The official beginning of Bush's presidency was on January 20, 1989, so that most of the actions in the novel take place during the first year of Bush's administration. The effects of Reaganomics are beginning to be felt, and Bush does not seem to be quite the president that Rabbit wanted. Although he was the only one among his Florida friends who actually voted for Bush, presumably because Bush represented continuity rather than change, he begins to realize that America is awakening from the Reagan anesthesia, and as his friend Bernie had predicted "when you come out of anesthesia, it hurts like hell" (62).

Bernie's remark seems to have come straight out of Anthony Lewis's article, "The Cost of Reagan," published in the *New York Times* on September 7, 1989. Lewis claims that like so many Americans (and Bernie) he also believed in the "it's morning again in America" slogan of Reagan's campaign. In September, after eight months under Bush, Lewis realizes how painful the legacy of eight years of Reagan has become. For him, too, it is like awaking from anesthesia—"it is the morning after." Lewis continues: "The reckoning is starting to come in for those eight years. We see that the indulgence of private greed exacted a heavy public cost, one that will burden our children and grandchildren"

(A27). Similarly, Jim Hanson writes that the debt of every American came to be $16,000 per capita and that the "federal debt alone exceed[ed] $4 trillion, which [was] more than half of the gross national product each year." Hanson also sees the Reagan era as responsible for what he regards as a major sign of the decline of the American empire—the transformation of America in a single decade from "the largest creditor nation to the largest debtor nation" in the world (6). Rabbit's observation about the feeling of being anesthetized during the Reagan days finds its counterpart in middle-American behavior. It is, for example, corroborated by consumer advocate Ralph Nader, who also claimed that the president "led the nation in a drunken world-record spending binge" (Gimlin 17).

Lewis's article reminds us that the self-indulgence policy has led to the S and L banks and HUD scandals, which are a constant presence in the news Rabbit reads, hears, and discusses and which will cost taxpayers billions of dollars. It also, argues Lewis, led to extravaganzas like James Watts's $300,000 telephone bill—all of which have created "hostility to the role of government" and diminished the common citizen's faith in political institutions.[6]

Rabbit, however, like at least 38 percent of Americans, has certainly not lost faith in political institutions. Although he realizes that foreign and national debt has increased and that scandals of all sorts have become as visible with politicians as with ministers of the church, he remains as conservative, nationalistic, and confident as President Reagan himself. He is a

---

[6] On August 9, 1989, President George Bush signed the S and L law, providing 50 billion dollars to close down or sell about five hundred insolvent or nearly insolvent savings and loan institutions (S and Ls). The evidence that Bush inherited the problem from the Reagan administration is that these institutions had lost $7.8 billion in 1987 and $12.1 billion in 1988, losses reported by the Federal Home and Loan Bank Board.

faithful disciple of Reagan's freshly recovered "new patriotism"—a feeling which is by nature incompatible with distrust of any national institution. Manifest loss of faith in the institutions belongs to another shade of the ideological spectrum—a shade which certainly does not define Rabbit or middle America. For him America will always be "the happiest . . . country the world has ever seen" (371), no matter what mistakes are made.

What is happening then is that Rabbit's anxiety and uneasiness have to do with his uncertainty about Bush's capacity to be the great leader Reagan was. As with Reagan, his feelings are ambiguous. He respects the man but cannot hide his disappointment at hearing the president's name on television being used in vain and robbed of its dignity. It hurts him, for example, to hear that Bush and his wife "[take] showers with their dog Millie" (295). This behavior makes them too human and is therefore inappropriate for someone in charge of running the country. He cannot help missing Reagan:

> At least he was dignified, and had that dream distance; the powerful thing about him as President was that you never knew how much he knew, nothing or everything, *he was like God that way* . . . With this new one you know he knows something, but it seems a small something. Rabbit doesn't want to have to picture the President and middle-aged wife taking showers naked with their dog. Reagan and Nancy had their dignity. (295, my emphasis)

As Rabbit sees it, the aura of dignity and power which Reagan had and which was the source of his authority is no longer there with Bush. He lost the stature which accompanies the presidential post by allowing himself to be vulgarized by the media. He looks smaller than Reagan. God's country, Rabbit thinks, needs a great president, a president who in some ways resembles God. As Stephen E. Ambrose observed about the Reagan days: "[The

American presidency has become] a symbol that is almost a monarchy" (Gimlin 17). Ambrose concludes, therefore, that the people's evaluation of the president is increasingly based not so much on his command of daily details and figures but on his symbolic capacity to inspire and to point out the direction that has to be traveled. As Peter B. Levy noted, Reagan came to be known as the "Great Communicator" not only because of his extraordinary ability to speak to the American public, but especially because he surrounded himself with a team of communications specialists who knew how to emphasize his strengths and hide his weaknesses. This practice explains why his chief of staff, James Baker III, would avoid scheduling press conferences and would instead promote Reagan's appearances in public ceremonies in which every action, every word, and every photo opportunity was carefully scripted, minute by minute. Baker knew that Reagan had a poor command of details but that he fully understood television's potential for communication, being able to deliver speeches "with poise and confidence rarely matched by other politicians" (Levy 175). Rabbit appropriates his president's lack of control over details during the Fourth of July parade when he plays the role of Uncle Sam. During the parade, Rabbit's frustration is that he cannot live up to people's expectations when it comes to details: "Strange people with puzzled Eighties faces keep asking directions, because he is dressed as Uncle Sam and should know. He has to keep telling them he doesn't know anything" (364). People somehow judge him as he judges the president, i.e., as a symbol—somebody who should know. Like the people, Rabbit realizes that, although the "symbol" may know very little, it remains inspiring.

His feeling thus is that the country under Bush is losing strength. He comments that "now that Bush is in . . . we are kind of on the sidelines . . . we're sort of like a big Canada, and what we do doesn't much matter to anybody else . . . It's a kind of relief, I guess, not to be the big cheese" (358). Rabbit makes this observation at the lot on June 19, 1989 (five months after Bush's inauguration), to Elvira, the salesperson Nelson hired.

Elvira's reaction to Rabbit's comment deserves our attention, for she quickly nationalizes Rabbit, perhaps perceiving that not only will he parade as Uncle Sam during the coming Fourth of July festivities but that he already feels he *is* Uncle Sam. Elvira promptly realizes that Rabbit's sentence has a meaning which Rabbit himself does not perceive. He is not talking about Bush at all, she correctly observes, but about himself: "You matter to everybody, Harry," she says, "if that's what you are hinting at" (358). Rabbit and the country are regarded as one and the same.

In fact Elvira's comment is just another textual device suggesting that we look at Rabbit as more than an individuality. Although a little heavier, he *is* in many ways the Uncle Sam that paraded down the streets of Mount Judge. In addition to the right physical build, he has the ideological components which make him adequate for the occasion. In this sense then he is transmuted into the collective; and like the collectivity to which he belongs, he has already, through his incredible capacity for adaptation, begun to appropriate the life of his new president. Bush's difficulties running the country become Rabbit's difficulties running his home; Bush's difficulty in paying the foreign debt becomes his difficulty in paying what Springer Motors owes the Japanese; and neither of them is, at the moment, "the big cheese." Under the circumstances Rabbit cannot help thinking, "Well, if doing nothing works for Bush, why not for him?" (477). The process of appropriation has begun. Not surprisingly, Rabbit reacts in much the same way Updike himself did in the nineties when, although disapproving of Bill Clinton, he defends his president: "All my indignation is basically against all the people that won't let the guy alone and be president. He won it fair and square . . . and it's a sad world when we're so happy to harass a public servant like this"(Garner 2). Updike's statement could well have come out of Rabbit's mouth. Like Rabbit and Alf Clayton, Updike "tends to like all presidents" (2), even little-revered ones like James Buchanan, by many considered the worst president the country has ever had.

As I shall demonstrate later, the end of the Cold War coincides with a time of increasing foreign presence in the country, especially in the economy, so that besides being robbed of his political motives, Rabbit is robbed of his sense of national economic stability. On December 27, 1988, Dimitri K. Simes states in an article called "If the Cold War Is Over, Then What?": "For more than 40 years, America's international strategy has been subordinated to one overriding concern—deterring Soviet global designs against the West." And he concludes that the "one-dimensional fixation on the East-West rivalry is no longer a credible option," suggesting a new, pragmatic approach to redefine America's role in the world (*NYT* A12). On the same day, James M. Markham writes an article entitled "Unpredictable Russians Boggle West's Brain" (*NYT* A2), in which he tries to determine the next moves of President Gorbachev. Although Reagan assured the nation that President Gorbachev was different from previous Soviet leaders and could be trusted, many Americans  thought closeness with the Soviet Union was a gamble. The only thing of which they could really be sure was that, as Reagan put it, "nothing is less free than pure communism" (*FA* 20).

Simes and Markham's interpretations of America coincide with Updike's interpretation of his own character. Updike reminds us that although the collapse of communism in eastern Europe happened late in the year of 1989 (the novel ends on September

22), Rabbit knows it is coming. As Updike once observed, "Like me, he has lived his life in the context of the cold war . . . and in some sense always justified, at the back of his mind, by a concept of freedom of America that took sharpness from contrast with Communism. If that contrast is gone, then that's another reason to put him, regretfully, to rest in 1990."[7] The fifties are over and the ideology which sustained them has to be put to rest, forcing middle America to redefine and redesign itself.

---

[7] Updike, John. "Why Rabbit Had to Go." In the *New York Times,* April 5, 1990.

# CHAPTER FOUR

## DEBT CRISIS AND THE JAPANESE INVASION

That is what I am also trying to do: to say what is changing in
the United States—through imagination, to tell the truth about
the U.S.

—John Updike, *Conversations*

Waking up from the Reagan anesthesia also meant waking up,
among other things, to the reality of foreign debt. As Rabbit appropriates Bush's plight, America is emblematized in the Springer
Motors dealership or, as Rabbit calls it, "the lot." The lot becomes
a microcosm of America, plagued by debt to foreigners—
completely at the mercy of foreigners—and administered by
"scatterbrains" who, like Janice and Nelson, "will just drift along
deeper and deeper into debt like the rest of the world" (431). Edward Vargo's finding among Updike's manuscripts at Harvard's
Houghton Library of a note reading "Natl deficit = Nelson's
debts" verifies that Updike intended us to see the lot as a symbol
standing for America (32).

Although Nelson insists that they owe very little money and, moreover, that Springer Motors has been underfinanced for years, Rabbit cannot help expressing his fears that the country has been taken by foreigners and that Americans are losing control: "We are drowning in debt! We don't even own our own country any more" (417). Earlier in the novel, Nelson predicts that in ten years the Japanese will "have bought the whole country. Some television show I was watching, they already own all of Hawaii and half of L.A. and Nevada. They are buying up thousands of acres of desert in Nevada!" (37).[1] We should recall that the Japanese presence in the United States became highly visible to common citizens precisely during the *Rabbit Is Rich* days of the seventies when the gas-saving Toyotas looked like salvation. The threat of Japanese economic power in the eighties, however, achieves added presence through numerous dramatizations on television. These dramatizations are obviously themselves an expression of the economic phenomena in action. It may be worth recalling that as early as 1987 America's foreign debt was eased by the borrowing of $1 trillion from the Japanese and others. The fear of the Japanese buying into America can be found in a large number of documentaries broadcast during the years 1987–1989. These documentaries stress that Japan is not only lending money to the United States but also buying into every sector of the American

---

[1] Nelson probably watched ABC's *20/20* documentary called "Buying Hawaii" which was aired on July 8, 1988, although many similar documentaries were aired as early as February 1987. A more recent and shorter report was aired by ABC on October 31, 1988, about Japanese control over major American cities, specifically citing Los Angeles. During their presidential campaign, Michael Dukakis and George Bush presented opposing views of this Japanese presence; the former expressing serious concern over foreign dominance, the latter claiming that markets need to be open. The population interviewed also showed ambivalent feelings, much like Rabbit's, some claiming that their jobs depended on the Japanese, others saying that there ought to be some restrictions on foreign investment.

economy. Japan is buying government bonds, stocks, Hollywood studios,[2] ballpark franks, record companies, computer chips, financial services, real estate, high-rise buildings, and universities, from Tennessee to California to New York. Furthermore, in 1989 Mitsubishi bought a majority share in the corporation that controls the Rockefeller Center in the heart of New York City.

A similar "scare documentary" was seen by Rabbit. His fears can be explained in part by the fact that America was throughout the decade the country in the world with the highest rate of foreign investment by far (Goyal C1). Some more visible materializations of this investment were the Japanese purchase of buildings in downtown Los Angeles, their buying of traditional American corporations, their presence in Hollywood, and as the *New York Times* edition of August 2, 1989, reported, their buying into ailing United States campuses[3] (having already bought part of a campus in Oregon and created the Salem-Teikyo University in Salem, West Virginia, among other aggressive initiatives).[4]

The lot as a microcosm of America operates in Rabbit's mind as a prefiguring of national economic disaster—a disaster caused by increasing national and international debt and by reckless spending. Springer Motors's loss of the Toyota franchise due to

---

[2] Of the five major Hollywood studios, three were purchased by foreign money in the 1980s or early nineties: Universal Pictures, later MCA, was taken over by the Japanese company Matsushita in 1990; Twentieth Century Fox was bought in 1985 by Rupert Murdoch and became a part of his Australian-based News Corporation Ltd.; and Columbia was purchased by Sony in 1989. The other two studios were saved by national mergers and acquisitions: Warner Brothers benefited from the merger of Time, Inc. and Warner Communications, Inc. (WCI), forming one of the largest communications companies in the world; and MGM, after selling its library to Turner Broadcasting System, merged with United Artists to form MGM/UA. In 1989 Quintex Corporation of Australia failed to obtain MGM/UA.

[3] It is probable that Rabbit is referring to the *Business World* documentary called "Japanese Course at Brigham Young" aired on August 21, 1988.

[4] In *New York Times*, August 2, 1989.

debt and poor administration is but an emblem or an omen of what Rabbit perceives might happen to his country.

Rabbit is definitely not alone in his concerns. From January 1987 to December 1989, over seventy documentaries were aired on American television dealing with the Japanese presence in America. The questions raised by these documentaries are frequently announced in their titles: "American Game, Japanese Rules," "Losing the Future," "Washington Debt," "Japanese Investment in the U.S.," "The Newest Japanese Export," "Semi-Conductors—Japanese Hegemony?," "Buying Hawaii," "U.S. Versus Japan on Copyright Differences," "Biotechnology—Will We Rise to the Japanese Challenge?," "America's Sellout," "Another Japanese Invasion," "Should Japan's Buying Spree Scare Us?," "Could a Bust on Wall Street Begin in Tokyo?," and "Who Owns America?" Each and every program poses enough questions to scare the most self-reliant American: How dangerous is Japanese domination of the microchip market? How will the trillion dollar loan from Japan be paid back? Is the Japanese buying spree good for America? Are the Japanese buying America's security? Will America win or lose? Will the Japanese dominate the market in high-definition television? These and other similar questions are so prevalent and so frequently asked in the national media that the historical references we find in Updike's text become in comparison little more than the tip of the enormous underlying ideological iceberg which composes the scene—a scene whose fear and xenophobia impregnate all agents, agencies, acts, and purposes.

Mr. Shimada, the Toyota representative, not only informs Rabbit of the cancellation of the franchise, but he also lectures him about the proper ways to conduct business. As we can see from the excerpt below, however, Mr. Shimada is not lecturing to Rabbit, the individual—he is lecturing to the American nation:

In recent times big brother act rike rittle brother, always cry and com-
prain. Want many favors in trade, saying Japanese unfair competition.
American way in old times. But in new times America make nothing, just
do mergers, do acquisitions, rower taxes, raise national debt. Nothing
comes out, all goes in—foreign goods, foreign capital. America take everything, give nothing. Rike big brack hole. (390)

What Mr. Shimada is saying can be read as the Japanese version, with a Japanese accent, of what concerned the Reagan and
Bush administrations in relation to foreign trade throughout the
decade. Japanese trade restrictions were the main topic of many
high-level meetings between officials of the two countries, with
officials frequently voicing their complaints about Japanese trade
practices. Considering the date Mr. Shimada makes his observation to Rabbit (i.e., in the first week of August), we could assume
that he is referring to the Bush administration's manifest intention
of citing Japan for unfair trade practices, expressed in late April
1989. The intention to file a complaint and to impose trade sanctions against Japan was the subject of television programs such as
"Japan in Crisis" and "Japan and Unfair Trade Practices": the first
aired on ABC's *Business World* on April 30, 1989; the second on
*Business World* on May 7, 1989. Just as Mr. Shimada's bill to Rabbit
covers a period ranging from November 1988 to May 1989, we
may assume that these particular references are again only the
visible part of the immense iceberg of the trade war. In fact, historical evidence confirms that one of the high points of the trade
war occurred as early as March and April 1987 when America
imposed trade sanctions on Japanese products containing semi-
conductor chips. High tariffs were imposed on these products as
an attempt to curb reported Japanese dumping practices and to
protect American industry. As the trade war heated up, Japanese
officials came to Washington for trade peace talks and negotiation

on the marketing of microchips. Thus Mr. Shimada's reference to
America as "rittle brother" who "comprains" all the time and
wants special favors in trade has as its source not just one incident
but the whole spirit of the American economic scene in the 1980s.
It should be recalled that the trade deficit was extremely high
throughout the decade, having increased from $24.2 billion in
1980 to $107.9 billion in 1984 to $152.1 billion in 1987. By 1989, the
first year of the Bush administration, the trade deficit had come
down to $109.6 billion. Similarly, the national debt increased
steadily during the Reagan-Bush years, starting at $1 trillion in
1980, increasing to $2.8 trillion in 1989, and reaching $4 trillion in
1992. It is not surprising, therefore, that Rabbit has the feeling that
America is no longer American and that the country is drowning
in debt and at the mercy of foreigners.

Mr. Shimada's reference to "mergers" also deserves a few
comments. It finds its clearcut rock-bottom equivalent in ABC's
*Business World* documentary aired on March 15, 1987, called
"Takeover Fever and Merger Mania"[5] and in the over two hundred fifty mergers and acquisitions which occurred during 1989,
many of them involving foreign capital. Mr. Shimada's view that
America is at a point where all goes in and nothing goes out, like
a "big brack hole," speaks directly to the fears of middle America
in general in those days—a fear aired on all major television networks and  materialized in such programs as "Foreign Invest-
ments in the U.S.,"[6] "U.S. Debt,"[7] "U.S. Trade Deficit,"[8] and
"Foreign Goods & U.S. Debt,"[9] just to name a few of the most
popular. The questions asked in these broadcasts invariably suggest that the United States is being financially infiltrated by for-

---

[5] Major question asked by the program: "Are mergers good for the economy?"
[6] Aired on February 1, 1987 (ABC's *Business World*).
[7] Aired on April 26, 1987 (ABC's *This Week*).
[8] Aired on September 13, 1987 (ABC's *Business World*).

eign countries, exporting jobs and money, and allowing itself to be dangerously flooded by foreign money and foreign goods.

Should Americans take foreign investment as a demonstration of confidence in their country? Should they be happy about it, or should they feel threatened by an imminent takeover? Rabbit has difficulty dealing with this uncertainty, especially because he seems to share Mr. Shimada's assumption that instead of being afraid of foreign competition and blaming others for their increasing economic problems, Americans should reexamine their own inadequate ways of conducting business. He has seen what Nelson's drug use, Lyle's AIDS, and poor administration overall have caused on the lot. The Angstroms' dealership, therefore, as a microcosm for the country, seems to be a perfect target for the outpouring of Mr. Shimada's petulance and impertinence.

The American trade deficit reached such critical heights during the Reagan years that in 1988 Congress enacted the Omnibus Trade and Competitiveness Act, authorizing the government to retaliate with high tariffs on Japanese imported goods if the Japanese restrictions on imported goods were not removed. Aware that economic interdependence required a solution which would benefit both countries, the American government devalued the dollar in relation to the Japanese yen to make American products more competitive, and Japan was persuaded to set voluntary quotas in its automobile and steel exports to the United States. But as Peter Levy notes, "the American appetite for Japanese goods remained very high. By 1989, Honda had become the best-selling car in America, and Japanese electronic goods, from videocassette recorders (VCRs) to stereo components, gained an even greater share of the American market" (214). Japanese-American relations improved only with the breakout of the Gulf War when Japan proved to be a financially useful ally.

---

[9] Aired October 4, 1987 (ABC's *This Week*).

Trade deficit and budget deficit also concerned the International Monetary Fund (IMF), which registered its complaint in April 1989. The American administration's projected budget deficit for that year was $162 billion, and the trade deficit was an estimated $135 billion—$35 billion less than it had been in the previous year. Both deficits were considered by the IMF to pose a danger to the growth of the world economy. By September 1989 the Bush administration could claim a small victory in its fight for trade deficit reduction. It announced that in July, because of the decline in imports, the trade deficit fell to $7.5 billion—the lowest in four-and-a-half years.[10]

Mr. Shimada's speech is then constructed as a Japanese answer to well-known problems that Americans were facing at the time. Mergers and acquisitions were rampant to the extent that the terminology suffused even the movies. In *Working Girl*, for example, a marriage proposal is made by saying "Let's merge," and the acquisition of a major radio network succeeds because of the threat of a supposedly imminent Japanese takeover. Although Mr. Shimada blames poor administration for America's present predicament, he tries to find a deeper and more meaningful explanation for this dire situation. As he continues with his lecture, he identifies as its ultimate cause the imbalance between the way Americans value discipline and freedom. For him, America is failing because there is too little *giri* (order, responsibility, obligation) and too much *ninjo* (freedom, human spirit). In America these two forces are said to receive disproportional value, *giri* having lost its relative importance. That is the reason why Toyota sees as its role the creation of "irands of order in oceans of freedom" (392). While blaming the *national* attitude for the present predicament, Shimada is also blaming Nelson and Nelson's father, who spends half the year "in Frorida, enjoying sunshine and tennis, while

---

[10] In *New York Times*, September 16, 1989.

young boy plays games with autos" (393). In other words, America's methods are failing because American citizens are placing excessive value on what has historically been one of the most precious of America's assets—individual freedom. Freedom has been pushed to such extremes, he believes, that it is leading Americans into self-indulgence, selfishness, and lack of group order. Again, Rabbit and America are regarded as one.

Rabbit's humiliating experience with Mr. Shimada and his disappointment at losing the Toyota franchise are briefly replaced by optimism when Janice suggests that they could reopen the lot as a family business, as it used to be before the Japanese and their money came in: "The idea of rebuilding the lot from scratch . . . excite[d] him" (398). In another demonstration that he sees himself as sharing the problems and concerns of the nation, Rabbit appropriates the hegemonic national attitude when considering the possibility of the lot's economic revival: "So they owe a few hundred thousand—the government owes trillions and nobody cares" (398). If the country can make it, so can Springer Motors.

What could be a solution for the lot could also be a solution for the country, and vice versa. But the idea of the whole world in debt and nobody paying—the United States, Mexico,[11] Brazil,[12]—is troubling and difficult to follow. International relations have become too complex for Rabbit, operating in mysterious ways; business has become so elaborate that he does not trust himself to analyze the books of Springer Motors, especially now that Lyle

---

[11] A special report on Mexico's foreign debt called "Debt Reduction for Mexico" aired on PBS's *Washington Week in Review* on July 28, 1989.

[12] In 1987 Brazil suspended all payments on its foreign debt, arousing concern whether the huge third world debt could lead the American bank system to a crisis. On March 1, 1987, the documentary "Brazilian Debt" was aired on PBS's *Adam Smith*. On September 27, 1987, the *Business World* documentary "Third-World Debt" discussed the meeting of international bankers in Washington, D.C. Debt repayments were at the top of their agenda.

has their accounts on computer diskettes. Somehow the global economy, with its intricate national and international network of operations, currency devaluations, tariffs, taxes, loans, interest rates, and mortgages, plays tricks which are transferred right into his home.

It is necessary to recall that throughout the year Secretary Nicholas Brady and Japanese delegates had been discussing ways of reducing the foreign debt of third world countries. The over $1.3 trillion debt owed by these countries was crushing their economies and threatening international economic stability. The idea was to ease this debt by providing financial support or indirect guarantees of interest payments to banks which accepted a reduction of the principal or of the interest rates on the loans made to third world countries. Mexico, Venezuela, and Brazil were the countries which would most likely benefit from this agreement. For Rabbit this is equated to having somebody else pay your debt for you; and this was precisely the resistance the plan met, for banks thought it would encourage debtor countries to avoid engaging in strong programs of economic recovery to meet their commitments. For the banks, up to the point of interruption of debt-service payments, it was more convenient to simply continue receiving payment of interest rather than the principal. This is one of the curious ways in which the historical scene is appropriated by Nelson in the novel. When Rabbit complains that everybody owes and nobody seems to have to pay, Nelson explains that the debt of the lot with Toyota has already been settled with a loan from:

> "Brewer Trust. A second mortgage on the lot property, it's worth at least half a million. A hundred forty-five, and they consolidated it with the seventy-five for Slim's five cars, which will be coming back to us pretty much as credit on the rolling inventory we were maintaining with

Mid-Atlantic Motors. As soon as they took our inventory over to Rudy's lot, don't forget, they started owing us."

"And you're somehow going to pay back Brewer Trust selling water scooters?"

"You don't have to pay a loan back, they don't *want* you to pay it back; they just want you to keep up the installments. Meanwhile, the value of the dollar goes down and you get to tax-deduct all the interest. We were underfinanced, in fact, before." (418)

To Rabbit's despair, Nelson, the unreliable former drug addict, seems to have it all worked out, much in accordance with what came to be called Reagan's "voodoo economics" and much in tune also with the creditors of third world debtor countries. Nelson's statement is dated August 28, 1989, a piece of information which only adds to his irresponsibility; for at this precise moment the dollar, which had been falling since 1987 and making American products more competitive in the international market, was on the rise against the West German mark and the Japanese yen— unlike it was in December 1988 when Nelson complained to his father about how expensive the "gas misers" or the "tidy little boxes" the Japanese call cars had become: "That's what hurts. The lousy dollar against the yen" (36). We could call Nelson a clever gambler, for he does not seem to be economically illiterate, but the precise placement of his statements in time adds to the identification of his behavior as irresponsible.

How much further into debt will Nelson drive them? Rabbit's feeling is that the Nelsons of America have already placed a second mortgage on the country—a country which he realizes is no longer his, as the lot is no longer his. Foreigners are everywhere— Japanese, Koreans, Italians, Mexicans, Cubans, Africans—all of them placing demands, giving orders, and complaining.

Rabbit's fear and xenophobia find their justification in the American scene of the 1980s, or at least in one possible reading of this scene. The massive presence of foreign money in America during the decade could be considered reason enough for fanning the flames of any nationalist. As David H. Blake and Robert S. Walters tell us in 1987:

> From 1973 to 1985 foreign direct investment in the United States increased from $20.5 billion to $183 billion. There is already more direct foreign investment in the United States than in any other country. The leading sources of foreign direct investment in the United States, by country of origin, are the United Kingdom, the Netherlands, Japan, Canada, Germany and Switzerland, respectively, and they account for almost 75 percent of the total. (92)

Rabbit, a common man, may not be aware of the statistics and of the specifics the data seem to reveal. Blake and Walters's observations may be startling to most Americans, even to American intellectuals. That the major portion of foreign money invested in the United States is not Japanese does not seem to match the national perception. Nor does it match Rabbit's perception, for whom, since the late seventies, it has become difficult to conceive of the lot or of America without the Japanese. What Rabbit seems to notice more, despite his professional respect for them, is the foreignness of the Japanese, their otherness. He views the Japanese much the same way as he views blacks and Mexicans, with the difference that they have money. His perception then comes less from the statistical evidence of foreign presence in the country than it does from the way this presence interferes with the life of white America and threatens to jeopardize its centrality. In this respect, considering Rabbit's white, Anglo-Saxon, Protestant cultural tradition, it is easy to understand why he would perceive non-central Europeans as posing a greater threat.

Even in hospitals Rabbit cannot avoid foreigners. At the hospital in Florida Rabbit's nationalism and xenophobia manifest themselves again as he gets irritated with Doctor Olman—an

Australian who, according to him, keeps attacking America: "If he doesn't like the food here, why doesn't he go back where he came from and eat kangaroos" (172). The irony of it all is that a foreigner is taking care of his very heart, his "typical American heart" (166).

Rabbit's enthusiasm to restart the business according to old American ways, national and independent, meets with reservations from Janice. As she sees it, they should not rush into things, for "everything is in flux" (398). To which Rabbit replies as usual: "I'm too old for flux" (398). The ongoing struggle finds its expression in the pain of readaptation and throughout the Rabbit novels becomes an endless fountain of tension between the protagonist and the world in which he lives.

Concerns like these which point to the death of an era and the birth of another find Rabbit unprepared. His mind, like the minds of middle Americans, is boggled by what is happening to the world and especially to his country. He finds it hard to understand the beginning of the end of communism; the end of the Cold War; the invasion of America by so many different races, colors, cultures, languages, and nationalities; the extensive internationalization of the American economy, with all these "scare documentar[ies] about foreigners buying up American businesses" (114); and the transformation of America into the leading debtor country. Somehow the death of the era is also the ominous foreshadowing of his own death, on its way to get him. But Rabbit is still moving, walking to "forbidden" places in the country, asserting his rights and insisting that he is not quite dead yet.

# CHAPTER FIVE

## THE THREAT OF FEMINISM

"Why do I keep writing about those phallocentric guys like
Rabbit Angstrom? I am a white male born at a certain time,
probably with some of the sexist baggage of men of my age
and vocation. But I can't believe that I'm a misogynist. Rather
the contrary."

—John Updike, *Salon* interview

Rabbit's life is an enactment of the major concerns of America in
the 1980s through the mind of the man in the middle. His world,
however, is not only plagued by communists, Arabs, Iranians,
Mexicans, Japanese, and other such external enemies. Internally,
Rabbit is beleaguered by three other destabilizing "enemies"—
feminism, AIDS, and drugs. These three enemies are another
source of Rabbit's distress. Day after day and with great intensity,
his life, like that of Americans in general in the eighties, is fusti-
gated by them and does not remain unaffected.

From the beginning to the end of *Rabbit at Rest* we sense that
the forces of feminism have acted upon the Angstrom couple.

Janice seems more in control of things. She participates in women's group meetings, studies, manages the family problems, runs Springer Motors during its time of crisis, and after twenty weeks of classes, becomes a salesperson. Throughout the novel she plays the roles of wife, mother, grandmother, and eager student, "trying," as she puts it, "to make something of what little life [she has] left" (317), or from Rabbit's point of view, "struggling so hard not to be dumb" (329).

Her group meetings are clearly changing her attitude toward life. She has come to the conclusion, after all these years with Rabbit, that "men are so fragile it turns out" (320). Rabbit sees her as more aggressive, more condescending, less herself, speaking with gestures that are not hers, using words that are not part of their common linguistic repertoire, and having grown a shell around her which "repels him" (6) and leaves him alone with his thoughts and premonitions.

Early in the novel Janice comes back from a women's group meeting exhibiting what Rabbit perceives as her "aggressive glow" (79) and tells him how awful men have been to women: "Oh, Harry, you men have been so awful! Not only were we considered chattel, but all those patriarchal religions tried to make us feel guilty about menstruating. They said we were unclean" (79). This realization seems to be the beginning of Janice's independence as a woman. She follows the general trend of her old friends Doris Kaufmann, Peggy Fosnacht, and Cindy Murkett, all of whom have or have had jobs, since "the women her age almost all do something now" (188). This is also an expression of a national trend. Statistical evidence shows that by 1983, 50 percent of the American workforce consisted of women. In 1970, 40 percent of the households consisted of husband, wife, and children under eighteen. In 1990 this traditional household was down to 26 percent. No wonder then that at the most trying moments in the novel, Janice will remember and make use of "the power her women's group in Florida talks about, the power men have always had" (315). Her action is not a simple imitation of male behavior, however; it is the dramatization of the increasing presence of women in the job market and in society in general.

It is clear also that the movie *Working Girl*, which Rabbit cannot watch to the end, has great influence on her decision to become a "working girl." To Rabbit's disbelief, Janice has barely come out of the movie theater when she announces: "I think I need a job. Wouldn't you like me better, Harry, if I was a working girl?" (107). The historical scene, thus, once again becomes an inseparable part of the story; and Janice, like Rabbit, becomes more than just Janice—she becomes an emblem for the time and space in which she lives as she appropriates the behavior of "all these women working in New York skyscrapers [who make her] so jealous" (113). Rabbit, we are told, "doesn't like [Janice's] idea at all" (107), but he doesn't give her a straight answer. Instead, hiding his impulse to beg her not to leave him, he asks her what she would do and where she would work and then changes the subject by asking about the movie's outcome, which he missed.

The outcome is economically summarized by little Judy, his granddaughter, as "the man from the wedding believed her story and she got an office of her own with a window and her nasty boss broke her leg and lost the man they both liked" (107). Not exactly a feminist perception, yet a very plausible one, especially because *Working Girl* lends itself to be read as more a woman versus woman conflict rather than a battle between the sexes. Judy's summary somehow has erased all the disrespect, deceit, and dishonesty played on Tess McGill by her previous male bosses and by her former boyfriend. She has also erased the rather oppressive, hopeless atmosphere in which the crowds of women in the movie work. What in the end stands out above all is the cruel dishonesty of a female boss toward her female secretary, inspired by a dispute over the same man (strong suggestions of which are found in Janice and Pru's mutual distrust regarding Nelson). The hardworking, creative, and determined secretary manages not to defeat men (not directly, at least) but rather another woman, receiving as her reward the man she loves and a job where she has an office of her own with a window.

It is not easy to determine what exactly in the movie makes Janice think that Rabbit would love her better if she were a working girl. There seems to be no direct evidence of this either in the movie or in the novel, especially because Jack Trainer (Harrison Ford) shows his dislike for unscrupulous Katharine Parker (Sigourney Weaver) despite the fact that she is a successful working woman. His love for Tess (Melanie Griffith) is possibly strengthened by his better knowledge of her qualities, but the fact that she is a working woman is certainly not a decisive factor in his liking her more or less. As for Rabbit's view on the matter, we know him well enough to believe that he would prefer to see Janice at home becoming a better cook and a less sloppy housewife. Janice's agenda is definitely not Rabbit's. She may like herself better for doing what she is doing, but it will definitely not make phallocentric Rabbit like her better—something which she, ultimately, seems to want. In Rabbit's mind we read that "he preferred her incompetent" (303).

Janice's suspicions that Pru may be making Nelson's drug problem sound worse than it actually is, are not motivated by motherly love only; they involve her understanding that women have their hidden agendas, so that what is said and done by women is not necessarily what is meant by them. Janice is led to consider that Pru may be motivated to overdramatize Nelson's problem by her awareness of the ephemeral quality of a woman's looks. Still operating on the assumption that looks are the greatest asset a woman may have in life, Janice is suspicious that her daughter-in-law may be trying to play tricks on her son: "If she is going to get herself another man she better move fast because her looks won't last forever" (247). Janice, strangely enough, also accuses Pru of getting herself pregnant because Nelson was once "a good bet" (247)—the precise accusation Rabbit's mother directed at Janice in the fifties. Janice has internalized the traditional evaluation of women as made by men to the extent that she adopts the same terms for evaluating other women without realizing that she is reinforcing and perpetuating the phallocentric perspective.

Janice, however, seems to know what she is talking about. She is at least in part correct in her evaluation. Only a few days after she mentions her suspicions that Pru might have a hidden agenda, Pru reveals to Rabbit: "I've wasted my life. You don't know what it's like. You're a man, you're free, you can do what you want in life, until you're sixty at least you're a buyer. A woman's a seller. She has to be. And she better not haggle too long. I'm thirty-four. I've had my shot, Harry. I wasted it on Nelson. I had my little hand of cards and played them and now I'm folded, I'm through" (344). Rabbit's attempt to comfort her finds no convincing intellectual support. Unable to deny the "truth" of Pru's astonishing confession, even though she is almost half his age, Rabbit operates through sympathy, trying to place both of them at the same level of general human suffering; for in a world without God, he perceives that "we are all trash, really" (344). Yet as he says this, he senses that his generalization will provide no comfort to Pru. Still unable to emphatically deny what Pru is saying (that is, that with men it *is* different, that men *are* potential "buyers" until they are sixty; and that women, once they have lost the splendor of their youth, are slowly moving beyond the level of desire), he tries to comfort her by pointing out that nothing is more precious than one's health. "At least you're healthy" (344), he says, while trying to make her see that, contrary to what she thinks, as far as he is concerned she still has "lots of cards" to play.

Pru is, however, the third woman who expresses to Rabbit this same idea in less than a month. A few days earlier he talked to his sister Mim, who told him over the telephone that being fifty for a woman is being "ancient. That's cow pasture. That's hang-it-up time . . . You don't get the stares any more, it's like you've gone invisible" (287). Judging by the way Rabbit has always acted towards women (i.e., with an almost uncontrollable desire to get into their pants, as Nelson accurately puts it), one cannot help inferring that he perceives Mim's, Pru's, and Janice's words as a true expression of the different predicaments of the two sexes.

Considering that Janice's age places her closer to the "necrotic rather than erotic" to use Judie Newman's expression (5), or almost "beyond desiring" (375) with "old age collapsing in upon her" (432), as Rabbit sees it, one wonders if her desperate search for a job is not merely a form of compensating for her waning looks by reengendering herself and trying to do something else— something which men like Charlie and Mr. Lister value. Her impulsive suspicion that Pru has a hidden agenda finds its justification not only in her protective motherly love for Nelson but also in her awareness that Pru still has an asset which she herself no longer has—the capacity to be physically appealing to men, to be thought of as "still interesting to men in that way" (433). No matter how important the content of what she has to say, for Rabbit "she's no Connie Chung, let alone Diane Sawyer" (299), a more attractive reality which renders her secondary. A trace of jealousy can be identified in Janice's discourse after Rabbit claims that Pru is good-looking. Janice makes it clear that, although she herself does not consider Pru attractive, men like Rabbit who "don't mind big tough women" (247) might be attracted to her. If indeed Janice's interpretation of Pru is equivalent to a projection of her own anxieties, then her eager determination to become a salesperson, even at the cost of selling their own home and having to move in with Nelson and Pru and her two grandchildren in a small house, can be read as a search for fulfillment and appreciation by escaping the limitations of a life based on marketable physical beauty.

*Working Girl*, however, may have had a more direct influence on Janice through its general atmosphere and argument. Tess is a woman who resents not being taken seriously and not being acknowledged as competent by her male bosses. What she finds appealing about Katharine is that "she takes me seriously . . . I think it's because she is a woman." The first meeting of the two women is remarkable, especially when we remember Katharine's penchant for self-reliance:

> *Katharine*: Who makes it happen?
> *Tess*: I do.
> *Katharine*: Who?
> *Tess*: I do.
> *Katharine*: That's right. Only then do we get what we deserve.
>
> (Wade 34)

It turns out Katharine is dishonest, and the reason she supposedly takes Tess seriously is strictly selfish. Tess, however, without a Harvard degree but hardworking and determined to succeed, functions as a source of inspiration as she discovers that to achieve success some rules have to be bent. As she tells Mr. Trask, her new wealthy boss: "You can bend the rules plenty once you get upstairs, but not while you're trying to get there. And if you're someone like me, you can't get there without bending the rules" (Wade 121). Tess's words and her practical accomplishment must have sounded encouraging for a beginner like Janice, showing her that despite the difficulty to overcome prejudice a woman can succeed in the workplace. Janice's excitement after seeing the movie may well have come from her identification with Tess's realization that she is no longer "the trusting fool" she was a week ago.

From his macho perspective Rabbit hates it all, quietly "blaming [women] for the world as it is" (98) and suppressing his impulse to help Janice with the household chores. He resents the food she prepares, for he feels Janice has evolved from the poor cook of earlier decades to "a great warmer-up of leftovers in the microwave, and a great buyer over at Winn Dixie of frozen meat-loaves and stuffed peppers and seafood casseroles in their little aluminum pans that can be tossed into the trashmasher dirty" (112). He resents the courses she is taking and especially her hunch that Mr. Lister, her teacher, likes her. He also resents Janice's admiration for the television show *Roseanne*, which, according to her, portrays a woman who is "fat and messy and mean, like most of the women in America" (384). He resents her not having time for him, even on his first day back from the hospital, because she has to take a quiz (throughout the story Janice spends twenty weeks out of thirty-five taking courses). He resents her going out with her classmates and her crowd of "know-it-alls" (189) and he resents her going out with their friend Charlie "to process," although it was he who suggested that Charlie talk things over with her. In short, Rabbit is afraid. He prefers Janice incompetent and unable to leave; he prefers her as he thinks she always was—his. His fear of losing her is also his fear of changing a lifestyle to which he has grown so accustomed that a little shift destabilizes him: "Much as Janice irritates him when she's with him, when she isn't in the room with him, or when he can't hear her knocking around in the kitchen or upstairs above his head, he grows uneasy" (222). To feel at ease he has to have her around the house, preferably in the kitchen or in the bedroom, although not even there can he think of her as deserving a passing grade (200). In his view, Janice will never cease to be a "tight little Protestant" (251) who will never get a grade over C even in home economics (200), no matter how hard she tries.

Interestingly, Rabbit also takes his view on the current state of family affairs from a French movie starring Gerard Depardieu that he sees on television, "about a man who comes to a village and usurps another man's identity, including his wife. In a moment's decision the young widow, besmirched and lonely, accepts him as her husband" (85). The movie, we discover, is *The Return of Martin Guerre* (1982) directed by Daniel Vigne, with Gerard Depardieu and Nathalie Baye in the leading roles. Based on fact, the story is about a sixteenth-century peasant who one day disappears from home without notice and after several years returns to his village and wife, literate and a much better and more pleasant person. The story line speaks both to Pru's wish that "Nelson would grow into somebody like Rabbit" (345) and to Rabbit's inner wish to escape his present predicament. Later in the novel, after Janice finds out that he has indeed "usurped" his son's lonely and ill-treated wife, he will once more attempt to escape. Unable to suppress his thoughts, conscious of the possible consequences of the materialization of his forbidden desires, and probably having the ending of the movie in mind (it turns out the man is a clever impostor and is hanged for it), Rabbit concludes that "there ought to be a law that we change identities and families every ten years or so" (85). Unable to forget the movie, he gets titillated by "the idea of a wife as a total stranger . . . as strange as a whore" (88). Thus, as with *Working Girl*, the historical scene is also appropriated by the characters and brought to bear directly upon their thoughts and actions, each of them reading into these movies their own anguish and desire for fulfillment.

Profoundly troubled by the direction the war between the sexes is taking, Rabbit adds to his uncontrollable sexism his also uncontrollable, almost genetic, anticommunism:

> They have jobs, money, even the young ones that used to be home making babies. If you look, more and more, you see women driving the buses, the delivery trucks. It's getting as bad as Russia; next thing we'll have women coal miners. Maybe we already do. (352)

In "Why Rabbit Had to Go," Updike points out that "the sense of being useless, of being pushed to one side by his wife and son," has a dimension similar to the end of the Cold War. Indeed, this seems to be the frame of mind which propels Rabbit's actions. His reasoning is similar to that of the president's: If Reagan can "get cozy with Gorby," why can't this Cold War between women and men come to an end as well? This is what, at times, he tries to do—never, nonetheless, overcoming the uneasy feeling that doing so violates his very nature. Rabbit in this respect is very much like Updike himself, who reminds us in the *Salon* interview: "In a way you're stuck in your own gender, and you have to sing your own song in the end" (Garner 2).

During his first visit to the lot Rabbit is surprised to discover that Nelson has hired Elvira Ollenbach as a car salesperson. He immediately feels the need to "control his face, so his chauvinism doesn't show" (209), even though hiring women and minority employees has become Toyota's policy. To strike up a conversation Rabbit reminds Elvira that "you don't think of it as a woman's game . . . women sales reps, I mean." Elvira, aware that Rabbit's view is the common view, answers: "I know, isn't that strange, when it is really such a natural?" (210). Her claim, however, that she makes female customers feel less intimidated and male customers less afraid to show their ignorance indicates that to a large extent she also carries within herself the typical gender stereotypes of her community. This internalization is perceived by Benny Leone, the other salesman on the lot. When asked by Rabbit to confirm how Elvira is really doing at her job, Benny replies that she is efficient "to a certain point, then gets rigid and lets the deal slip away. Like she is afraid the rest of us will say she's too soft" (212). Elvira is later recognized by Toyota as a competent and reliable salesperson and is actually invited by the new Brewer Toyota representatives to work for them. Yet Benny's observations only confirm Elvira's own self-consciousness about the way she deals with people. Although his perception points to the changing times, it also shows that in the eighties a long way still has to be traveled until the job Elvira does can be done by a woman without feeling conspicuous.

Rabbit meets Elvira again two months later in mid-June. This time he strikes up a conversation by taking out the daily paper and raising the abortion issue. He makes reference to a piece of news in the paper telling of four men chaining themselves to a car in front of an abortion clinic. He does it because "he knows where she stands: pro-choice. All these independent bimbos are. He takes a pro-life tilt to gall her but his heart isn't really in it" (353).

In fact the discussion brings back to his and the reader's memory his pro-life stand in the fifties when he begged his lover Ruth not to have an abortion. Although Ruth wanted to make him believe she had the abortion, he still thinks she had the baby and that he is the father of Annabelle Byer. Even knowing that he is not alone, that Reagan and Bush[1] and their followers stand with

---

[1] On January 23, 1989, President Bush addressed the March for Life, an anti-abortion rally in Washington, D.C., by telephone. He promised the 65,000 member audience that he would do his best to change the 1973 Supreme Court decision which legalized abortion in the United States. He called legalized abortion an American tragedy.

him on the issue, as time passes Rabbit becomes more and more confused, not so much because he is convinced by Elvira's arguments but because he perceives that the war with women will lead him nowhere.

It should be remembered that on Sunday, April 9, 1989, an estimated 300,000 people marched in a pro-choice rally in Washington, D. C., with abortion becoming more than ever before a crucial issue for the feminist movement and for women's rights. Although a *New York Times*/CBS poll on April 26, 1989, pointed out that the nation was sharply divided, it became clear that feminists felt stronger than ever after the April 9 march by advocates of free choice. As actress Marlo Thomas pointed out in the *New York Times* edition of April 10, "To those pontificators who relegated our movement to the ash-heap of post-feminism, I say, eat your heart out. The feminist generation that supports a woman's right to choose an abortion has reproduced."

The underlying controversy of the rally can be seen on the buttons, T-shirts, and banners carried by the marchers. They announced, among other things: "My body, my baby, my business," "Keep your laws off my body," and "Mother of two by choice." As Gloria Steinem, one of the feminist leaders of the march, declared, "We are marching here to ask, is the Supreme Court going to affirm that women are full citizens and not a property, or is the Supreme Court the captive of the extreme right wing?"(*NYT* April 10, 1989). Judging from the news, the April 9 march was among the most important feminist events of the decade.

The march did not, however, remain unquestioned. As expected, counter-demonstrators also showed their presence, chanting "Life! Life! Life!" They also rallied in many other parts of the country—in Washington, Seattle, Los Angeles, California, and especially Ocala and Fort Myers, Florida, where two abortion clinics were destroyed by arson the same day. These anti-abortion attacks on clinics reached their peak around June 20, 1989, when the *New York Times* reported that Connecticut militant abortion protesters literally clogged the state's jails. In just one incident that day two hundred sixty-one protesters were arrested for disrupting normal activities, breaking in, and damaging equipment. By July 3 a divided Supreme Court passed down a ruling which stopped short of overturning the historic 1973 *Roe v. Wade* decision.[2] While pro-life activists thanked the Supreme Court and hailed the decision as the dawning of a new era, Molly Yard, the president of the National Organization for Women (NOW), and Kate Michelman, from the National Abortion Rights Action League, made it clear that politicians opposing choice would no longer receive votes from members of their respective organizations. In a clear reference to President George Bush, who accord-

---

[2] The reference is to the historic January 22, 1973, Supreme Court ruling that abortion was a private matter between a woman and her doctor in the first three months of pregnancy. That decision was now threatened to be overturned by the Supreme Court. The statement was made prior to the Supreme Court's hearing of the Missouri abortion case in which an abortion clinic challenged the Missouri law which prohibited state funding of abortions. Missouri's appeal challenged the Supreme Court's 1973 *Roe v. Wade* decision and had the support of President George Bush, who not only vowed to veto federal funding of abortions for victims of rape and incest but also named an anti-abortion candidate for surgeon general. The abortion rights issue became highly politicized and ceased to be a matter of judicial decision. The Supreme Court started the hearings on April 26, with resultant pro-choice and pro-life demonstrations throughout the country. The likely positions of all justices were widely discussed, especially those of the three conservative Reagan appointees. Only on July 3 did the Supreme Court decide not to override the *Roe v. Wade* determination but to grant states the right to regulate abortion—which merely transferred the battle to another political sphere. All mayoral and gubernatorial elections that followed had, as a consequence, abortion as one of their major topics. Pro-choice activists, especially the National Organization for Women (NOW), didn't like the ruling and considered the decision a war against women. NOW preached that abortion should remain a federal constitutional issue. Pro-life groups, on the other hand, claimed victory, and although not completely satisfied with the Supreme Court's decision, understood it as a protection of the rights of the unborn: "We are smiling; our thumbs are up; and we feel that a new era is dawning," said one of the pro-life activists on television.

ing to Rabbit is "just as bad, anti-choice, [as the Pope]" (358), Michelman announced on the CBS *Evening News* on July 3: "To politicians who oppose choice we say: 'Read our lips; take our rights; lose your jobs.'" Michelman's expression, "read our lips," was obviously an appropriation of George Bush's major punch line against his opponent Michael Dukakis during the 1988 presidential campaign: "Read my lips: no new taxes!" Rabbit's Jewish friend Joe Gold, it should be recalled, similarly brings Bush's pledge into their political discussion during the golf game played in Florida. Ironically, to the astonishment of Democrats and Republicans, George Bush reneged on his famous pledge on June 26, 1990.

It is within this context of national conflict and international rapprochement with the enemy, the Soviet Union, that Rabbit and Elvira have their discussion of abortion on Monday, June 19, 1989. While discussing with Elvira the retirement of baseball heroes Mike Schmidt and Pete Rose, Rabbit thinks that perhaps an "alliance with this female" would be better than an argument. He is, however, "torn between a desire to strike an alliance . . . and an itch to conquer her, to put her in her place" (352). He ultimately prefers the alliance because it will not "rock the agency worse than it was being rocked" (352). In other words, Rabbit is not convinced by the feminist or pro-choice view—he just realizes that learning how to deal with the issue is a matter of convenience and perhaps survival, a forced "loyalty to the changing times" (212). The fact is that the feminism of the 1980s has spread its roots all over America and in one way or another has touched everybody.

What we know for sure is that the likes of Rabbit did not participate in the April 9 march in Washington, and if they did, they were among those few hundreds shouting "Life!" rather than among the hundreds of thousands shouting "Choice." The pro-choice perspective on the abortion issue, being a feminist issue *par excellence*, is a destabilizing factor in society—something for women who refuse the traditional bibelot treatment and cherish their independence. Rabbit, a lover of the old order and of stability, sees the increasing feminist presence as a threat to masculine dominance. Whereas Janice is trying in her own confused and prejudiced way to find out how the world works, Rabbit is stuck—and jealous because he is stuck. As he tells Thelma, "without her, I'm shit. I'm unemployable. I'm too old. All I can be from here on in is her husband" (207). And with Mr. Lister and Charlie around even that role is in danger.

To a large extent we could say that Rabbit is stuck because he cannot outgrow his view of women as objects of sexual pleasure, with instinct playing a very strong role in his life and frequently predominating over rational action. One only has to think of the many moments in the novel when Rabbit sees, meets, or thinks about women to perceive the extent to which sexual instinct drives him. The same way he is annoyed when the "cocoa-brown black chick" (4) driving a red Camaro convertible passes him without even a sideways glance, he regards it as a woman's duty to give him what he needs when he needs it—generally, sex. His description of Thelma as "the one person who for these last ten years has given him nothing but what he needed. Sex. Soul food" (197) is indicative enough of his way of behaving and of how essential sex is in his life. All women are, for him, objects of desire—the waitress in the restaurant, the nurses in the hospital, the female sales representative at the lot, his daughter-in-law Pru, etc.—unless they have grown "beyond desiring," in which case they become like Thelma, a burden, and have to be "unloaded" (238). At age fifty-six, Rabbit has his mind filled with memories of women with whom he had sex in the past (Peggy Fosnacht, Thelma, Ruth, the whore in Texas, his girlfriend Mary Ann) and those with whom he so badly wanted to have sex in the past

(Cindy Murkett and Melanie, his son's girlfriend). And because he vicariously enjoys all sexual possibilities represented by women around him, he sees Vanna White, the *Wheel of Fortune* star, as somebody who "makes you proud to be a two-legged mammal" (400). Not even little Judy, his granddaughter, escapes his phallocentric mind: "Some men some day will use that tongue" (130), he thinks. Rabbit is definitely convinced that "we've been programmed to tits and ass" (471)—a notion which is at the very basis of his conflict with women, men, and homosexuals alike. No wonder then that he cannot play the role of father-in-law and control his instincts to avoid the incestuous relations with Pru.

Rabbit also lacks the self-confidence to be able to do for Janice or for women in general what Charlie did for Melanie, who we are told became a doctor and still keeps in touch with Charlie because "she still had a bit of that poor-little-me-I'm-only-a-girl thing. I gave her the boost she needed" (236), Charlie explains. Doing for Janice what Charlie did for Melanie would destroy Rabbit's middleness, his true identity, an identity which may look old-fashioned but which is his nonetheless—always a step behind the progressive forces of history, always looking for adaptation rather than change. In the social scene of the eighties Rabbit represents a force which is being overwhelmed by the growing presence of feminism; he is slowly becoming old-fashioned and is terrified. His horror of the forthcoming changes is expressed in his dream at the Best Western motel north of Baltimore during his journey south:

> In his dream he is back at the lot, with a young woman who seems to be in charge. She wears a white cap and dangly earrings but when he leans close and tries to explain himself to her, to convey his indispensable usefulness to the enterprise, contrary to what she may have heard from

Janice, she makes a wry mouth and her face melts under his eyes in a kind of visual scream. (441)

In other words, Rabbit feels he is being replaced, displaced, and declared useless by the overwhelming presence of women. His death, therefore, becomes emblematic of the death of an era— the era of male domination in America. He is dying because his world is dying. The 1950s are definitely over, but Rabbit, having absorbed the sixties better than Janice (who still feels guilty about how she behaved then) and having cleverly survived the seventies by helping Toyotas sell themselves, finds it hard to believe that change is necessary or advisable. In fact he seems to reproduce the Depardieu movie he watched in which a character receives a shower of approving laughter when he mentions that if women were to fight our wars and command our lives, it would be the end of the world. Similarly, why should Rabbit change if his views can also still receive loud approving laughter throughout the country? Why should he change if, with all the others who think like him, he can still elect the nation's president? Middleness may have to be slightly redefined in the coming years. It will certainly have to make room for the increasing presence of women in every aspect of American life, but the old ideology of male dominance is definitely not dead yet.

# CHAPTER SIX

## THE THREAT OF DRUGS

I'm not responsible for the modern world. I'm just a portrayer of it.

—John Updike, *Conversations*

Coke is it, Judy sings.

—John Updike, *Rabbit at Rest*

Drugs and AIDS have become Rabbit's nemesis. They have ruined his business, thrown him into debt, affected his sex life, shattered his family, changed the social habits of his hometown, disgraced some of his athlete heroes, corrupted the police, shamed him with the Japanese, and threatened to drain the energy of the nation. As one of Rabbit's Jewish friends puts it, one has the impression that the younger generations have decided to take "a chemical short-cut" (58) in their pursuit of happiness.

Early in the novel we suspect that Nelson is a drug addict, and worse, that he might be infected with AIDS. Rabbit's mind as usual brings another story into the story, one he read in *People* magazine on Rock Hudson's death. "One of the first signs of AIDS" (50), he tells us, is the nose always running. Despite Rabbit's and Pru's fears, Nelson turns out to be HIV-negative.

He is, however, a drug addict—yet another in a city where "coke whores [are] all around" (434), where doctors are prescribing illegal drugs to athletes (384), and in a country where according to President George Bush "drugs have strained our faith in our system of justice; our courts, our prisons, our legal system are stretched to the breaking point. The social costs of drugs are mounting. In short, drugs are sapping our strength as a nation, turning our cities into battle zones . . . murdering our children" (*HD* 502). Governmental research indicated that an estimated eight million people used cocaine in 1988,[1] so that the scene described by the president slowly writes itself into the life of the Angstrom family.

While visiting Rabbit and Janice in Florida Nelson remains out of sight, doesn't participate in family outings, and hardly stays at home. Indications, soon confirmed, are that Nelson is driving around Miami looking desperately for drugs. As Thelma tells Rabbit a few months later:

> You must know about Nelson. My boy says he's a cocaine addict. They have all used it, that generation, but Nelson they tell me is really hooked. As they say, the drug runs him, instead of him just using the drug. (201)

Thelma's revelation is important in many ways. First, it indicates that the drug problem is not only Nelson's but his generation's, suggesting that even her own sons may be addicts (her

---

[1] A study conducted by Eric Wish, a visiting fellow at the National Institute of Justice, estimated that governmental surveys may have not counted the majority of regular users of crack and cocaine. Wish's findings were reported in an article by David Whitman published in *US News & World Report*, March 5, 1990.

sons later declare that they had indeed been taking drugs); second, it shows that drug addiction becomes an especially serious problem when, as is Nelson's case, the drugs run the individual, determining his actions and guiding his life; and third, it confirms what Rabbit suspected all along, namely that the Springer Motors accounts which Nelson showed him could not possibly be correct (with unexplained spending probably behind Pru's complaints that they had no money to pay their bills). Rabbit's long experience at the lot tells him that the sales reports do not follow the historical pattern of behavior of the average buyer. Partly because of his heart attack and partly because of his permanent conflict with his son, Rabbit had been spared the details about Nelson's addiction (his wife Janice knew very well what was happening since at least December 1988).

At the moment Rabbit has his first heart attack Janice is having a serious talk with Nelson on the subject of drugs. He tells her about the threats he has been receiving from drug pushers—threats which are actually confirmed months later in Pennsylvania when Rabbit receives similar phone calls. They have been threatening to "break [his] legs; . . . kidnap [his] kids [and do] physical harm to Nelson [and] to certain of his near and dear" (229).[2] During Janice's talk with her son, he tells her he owes drug dealers about $12,000, an amount which Janice is willing to give him if he promises her to stay "clean," much as George Bush is willing to spend $7.9 billion in 1990 ($2.2 billion more than what was spent in 1989) to see his plan succeed and to rid the country of drugs.[3]

---

[2] A number of television programs were aired in 1988 prior to Nelson's confession to his mother relating the effects of violence and drugs on families. Of these programs, perhaps the most remarkable was "Innocent Victims of the Drug Wars" aired on *Geraldo* June 9, 1988.

[3] In 1991 the drug war appropriated $11 billion, an increase of almost 40 percent over the previous year.

As it turns out, the debt of the lot is much higher than the figure Nelson quoted his mother—over $200,000—forcing Janice to consider selling their own house to pay it and avoid bankruptcy. To Rabbit's despair, "Springer Motors . . . went up in coke and pills for a queer" (406), and he cannot forgive his son for it, even after all evidences seem to indicate that Nelson managed to get rid of drugs. "Tell me, Nelson," he asks, "I'm just curious. How does it feel to have smoked up your parents' house in crack?" (481).

Drugs and AIDS clearly run hand in hand in the novel, the reader being constantly reminded that drugs (especially intravenous drugs) and AIDS are closely connected. As Nelson tells his mother: "I'll never go near a needle. That you can count on. Jesus, you can get AIDS that way" (146).[4] It is Nelson's importance as a character which gives the drug problem an even greater relevance in the novel than AIDS, although both are undoubtedly major issues of the 1980s and should be regarded as part of the same social disease. It should also be recalled that drugs and AIDS made the news throughout the decade and that drugs were present with particular intensity during 1989, the time in which most of the novel's action takes place and the year in which the war against drugs began to be fought on various fronts with a repressive apparatus of unprecedented strength. The significance of the issue may be perceived in the astounding number of entries in the *Television News Index and Abstracts* from April to December 1989:

---

[4] On July 25, 1988, the program "Dirty Needles and the Spread of AIDS" was aired on ABC's *Nightline*, discussing the distribution of clean needles to drug addicts as a possible way to stop the spread of AIDS. A similar program was aired on October 13, 1988, on *48 Hrs.* George Bush's speech also mentions the threat of dirty needles: "When four-year-olds play in playgrounds strewn with discarded hypodermic needles and crack vials, it breaks my heart" (502).

| | |
|---|---|
| April ......................... | 32 |
| May ......................... | 9 |
| June ......................... | 34 |
| July ......................... | 33 |
| August ..................... | 205 |
| September .............. | 279 |
| October ................... | 75 |
| November ............. | 45 |
| December ............... | 102 |

Not surprisingly, although the presence of the issue is high throughout the year, in August and September the media flooded the American public with information on the topic. George Bush's expected "war on drugs" speech was certainly the determining factor.

Nelson's drug addiction turns out to be much more serious than his parents could have imagined. To use George Bush's expression, in Nelson's case drugs are no "harmless recreation." Not only does he owe drug dealers a great deal of money but he is beginning to lose control of himself. As if emerging from the many television programs on drugs of the time, Rabbit identifies his drug-addict son as "shifty and jumpy, and kind of paranoid" (223); Judy says that "Daddy thinks ants are crawling over him" (252); Pru explains that "he's always feeling itchy" (252); and Nelson insists that when he went after Pru it was "like a monster or something had taken over my body and I was standing outside watching and felt no connection with myself. Like it was all on television" (261). On television the effects of drug addiction were indeed presented very much like that. Programs such as "An Anatomy of an Addict,"[5] and "How to Tell If Your Kid's on

---

[5] Aired on *Geraldo* on May 5, 1988, and repeated on August 30, 1988.

Drugs"[6] are only two examples of what could be found in the media at the time, trying to make the identification of addicts easier. Perhaps the most remarkable example of this attempt was that of Adelaide Sanford from the New York State Board of Regents who claimed during a meeting on the drug curriculum for state schools that there was a connection between skin pigmentation and drug addiction. The controversy was explored on *Like It Is* on April 9, 1989, in a program called "Adelaide Sanford and the Melanin Controversy."[7]

Nelson's addiction, as if emanating from the reality portrayed by the many television programs of the decade, makes him aggressive to the point of attacking his wife and children physically. In a redramatization of similar real life family conflicts portrayed on television in November 1988 and January 1989, Updike has Pru pushed to the verge of despair. One night in April, at 2:00 A.M., Pru calls Janice and Rabbit for help. It is difficult to determine the extent to which television programs and newspaper reports of the time were consciously employed and transformed by Updike in this particular instance, but following the general constructive trend of his method it becomes obvious that the actions here are, to say the least, appropriations of a materiality which suffused the American scene of the last years of the decade.

As would be normal to expect after the president's speech claiming that drugs are to a large extent the result of an attitude of American tolerance, Janice and Rabbit try to find explanations for the strange behavior of their son. Unavoidably they are led to think that maybe they have a share of responsibility not only for the boy's short stature but perhaps also for his addiction. Janice

---

[6] Aired on *Geraldo* on November 1, 1988.

[7] Adelaide Sanford, a member of New York's Education Policy-Making Board, claimed that a pigment in black skin bonds with narcotics, leading to drug abuse. Sanford, who is black, believed that this possibility should be studied.

blames herself for having left home in the sixties to live with her lover Charlie Stavros. She still cannot forget the image of Nelson with his bicycle standing for an hour in front of the apartment where she was with Charlie, looking up at their windows. She would see him and hide and not talk to him until, exhausted, he would leave. When Rabbit tells Janice that he was taking care of Nelson, he is reminded that he was doing so with the help of Skeeter, the black Vietnam veteran, and Jill, the hippie girl who died when his house caught fire. Although Rabbit does not refuse to take the blame for Nelson's drug addiction, he does not accept full responsibility for it either.

The reader cannot help recalling that Nelson's first exposure to the world of drugs was in the presence of his father twenty years earlier. In this respect, one might be tempted to see Rabbit as reproducing the guilt-free father who gave a marijuana joint to his daughter as a present on her thirteenth birthday, portrayed on CBS's *60 Minutes* on July 12, 1987. Yet we know that Rabbit in the sixties, despite a temporary flirtation with hippies, was the embodiment of the "solid citizen," and he should not be confused with a die-hard hippie of the eighties. Drugs scare him, not only because of the danger they represent to the lot and to the nation, but more simply because in his frame of mind it is difficult to accept that a man could act selfish "for a little white powder" (302). Were it for a woman Rabbit would more easily understand it.

Early in the novel, however, Rabbit does admit to himself that "the boy's trying ever since that business with Jill twenty years ago to protect women against his father. His son is the only person in the world who sees him as dangerous" (49) and as "an old juvenile delinquent" (71). Although Nelson is old enough to take his life in his own hands, he cleverly tries to use the knowledge he has of his parents' questionable past behavior to play the role of the helpless victim. The reader knows, however, that he is neither innocent nor helpless. The reader also knows that Rabbit's and Janice's behavior indeed had much to do with his education in the art of victimhood. The fact that all of them are partly right and partly wrong only adds to the complexity of their relationship, making them consequently appear true to life.

In 1989 Rabbit (like most Americans, according to the *New York Times*) seems to be in a punitive mood, having transformed early tolerance for drug use into condemnation. Were it not for Janice, instead of having Nelson sent to a rehabilitation clinic—which for him sounds like a thing communists would do—he would have called the police. In 1989 Rabbit epitomizes what President Bush referred to as the "zero tolerance [of] an angry America" (507). In fact, George Bush's war plan on drugs came at a time when a Gallup poll revealed that 27 percent of the adult population considered drugs as the most serious problem facing the nation— "eclipsing poverty, the economy, the environment and fear of war" (*NYT* September 3). The plan had as its major strategy a combination of law enforcement, international aid, protection of national borders, treatment of drug addicts, education, and prevention programs. The goal was to make the drug-free America proclaimed by Reagan become a reality.[8]

It is not surprising then to find that the story incorporates not only the mood of the times, but also its vocabulary and topical events. Bush's war on drugs and all that led to it become part of what Updike likes to call "the daily doings of ordinary people," including the domestic violence, the threats of dissatisfied dealers, violence on the streets, the use of drug addicts' slang words by school children, and the burning need to verbalize the anxiety

---

[8] This is how Peter B. Levy referred to the Reagan-Bush effort against drugs: "Despite much fanfare, money spent, high-profile arrests and convictions, and the doubling of the prison population, the Reagan-Bush years concluded without a victory in the war" (381).

surrounding the issue. In talk after talk Rabbit, Pru, and Janice need to bring up the subject. It has become part of their lives.

While Rabbit has lunch with Charlie, for example, the topic shifts from female sexuality to punk girls to the change in values that seems to be occurring. For punks, Charlie argues, "ugly is beautiful"(240), to which Rabbit responds with yet another visible change in the local mores. He mentions his drive around Brewer a few days earlier when he saw "some of these Hispanics were practically screwing on the street" (240). The discussion shifts quickly to drugs, for Charlie sees drugs as responsible for this behavior. Rabbit's contribution follows immediately, and it comes directly from the media. The passage merits being quoted in full because of the clear way the historic becomes the fictional as the public experience is appropriated by the life of a private citizen:

> "Did you see in the *Standard*, some spic truck driver from West Miami was caught over near Maiden Springs with they estimate seventy-five million dollars' worth of cocaine, five hundred kilos packed in orange crates marked 'Fragile'?"
>
> "They can't stop dope," Charlie says . . . "as long as people are willing to pay for it."
>
> "The guy was a Cuban refugee evidently, one of those we let in."
>
> "These countries go communist, they let us have all their crooks and crackpots . . ."
>
> "That's the other thing preying on my mind. I think Nelson is into cocaine."
>
> Charlie nods and says, "So I hear." (240)

The passage is one more rich example of history writing itself into fiction, ceasing to be simply background for the story. No longer is the story merely immersed in history or set against a historical background—it actually grows out of, or from, or because of history. Cuban involvement with drug trafficking was recognized by President Fidel Castro himself in June 1989. According to Cuban officials, Arnaldo Ochoa Sanchez, a Cuban revolutionary hero, helped to smuggle six tons of cocaine and marijuana from Colombia to the United States during 1987 and 1988. Sanchez was facing military trial for drug trafficking and corruption in Cuba during 1989.[9] In other words, Updike's transformation of the Cuban involvement in drug trafficking into fictional material serves the purpose of adding sharpness to the ideological definition of his protagonist. Updike has Rabbit see what he has been ideologically trained to see during the Cold War, namely, communist conspiracy against the United States in all corners of the globe. The selection of this piece of news out of a world of possibilities is a good example of Updike's deneutralization of historical material.

As with all the previous cases, it is not all history which serves the story. It has to be preferably that particular history, that particular topical event, that scene which serves the purpose of portraying the predominant ideological makeup of the characters, especially Rabbit's ideology. In other words, the piece of news selected *in casu* had to have as its protagonist a drug trafficker who, because of his foreignness, race, language, and political ideology threatens white capitalist America and what it stands for.

It is interesting to observe once more how Rabbit sees foreigners as responsible for the disruption of established mores, how he treats Hispanics derogatorily, and how the drug problem is easily transformed into a possible international communist plot to destabilize the country. For Rabbit drugs are something planted by "foreigners" of all kinds, be they Latin Americans, communists, or African Americans. The origin of the stress on Latin America can clearly be seen in the emphasis placed by the Bush administration

---

[9] Sanchez and three more army officers convicted by court-martial of conspiring to smuggle drugs into the United States were executed on July 14, 1989, six days after being condemned to death.

on the control of the supply of drugs, especially on countries such as Colombia, Peru, Bolivia, and Panama. Mexico, Honduras, El Salvador, Cuba, and Brazil are not excluded. All Latin American countries are considered either potential sources of the drug supply or outposts of the international drug cartels.

Similarly, Rabbit's assumption that criminals and drug addicts are mostly African Americans ["must have been black" (9) or "these druggy kids you deal with, they all black?" (407)] and the narrator's assumption that a white man walking in a black neighborhood must be "after some crack" (490) may have their explanations in the historical racism still prevalent in the country. Rabbit's Jewish friend Joe Gold seems to have no doubt about it. When explaining why the Republicans got the anti-black vote during the last presidential election when George Bush defeated Michael Dukakis, Joe is emphatic: "Face it: the bulk of this country is scared to death of the blacks. That's the one gut issue we've got" (61). A direct justification of this attitude may be found in the national racial orientation, of which the tremendous amount of evidence produced by the media is a clear example. As a rule, the media have portrayed African Americans as the major consumers and dealers of drugs in all major American cities, even in the nation's capital. Were one willing to argue about the neutrality of quantity, it would still be impossible to affirm that Rabbit's assumption is merely an expression of the overwhelming numbers of identified facts and not also a manifestation of the ideological charge carried by these facts. The overall impression which remains both from the media news and from Rabbit's observations is that essentially the nationality of drugs is Latin American, the color is black, and the ideology is communist.

If we recall how the dialogue quoted above started, with Rabbit trying to seduce the waitress at the restaurant, and if we remember for an instant his way of relating to women in general,

is that essentially the nationality of drugs is Latin American, the color is black, and the ideology is communist.

If we recall how the dialogue quoted above started, with Rabbit trying to seduce the waitress at the restaurant, and if we remember for an instant his way of relating to women in general, we may add sexism to his nationalism, anticommunism, racism, and xenophobia. These are the means used by Rabbit to reaffirm his power over a dominion he is afraid to lose.

At times we are led to believe that Rabbit, who always is trying to find a profound meaning for the news he hears and sees, is not aware of the history he verbalizes and appropriates. An instance of this seeming ignorance may be found in a dialogue which takes place during the night Pru called for help:

> "Nelson, when will it end?" Janice asks, tears making her voice crack, just from looking at him . . ."You must get off this stuff."
> "I am, Mom. I am off. Starting tonight."
> "Ha," Harry says.
> Nelson insists to her, "I can handle it. I'm no addict. I'm a recreational user."
> "Yeah," Harry says, "like Hitler was a recreational killer." It must be the mustache made him think of Hitler. If the kid would just shave it off, and chuck the earring, he maybe could feel some compassion, and they could make a fresh start. (260)

One interesting point about this passage is that drug addiction has become such a problem in the country that addicts can already be classified into various categories. This would only confirm what the news was saying all along, namely that drugs are widely available in American cities. It would confirm the sentence which the *New York Times* chose as its quotation of the day on September 8, 1989: "He can't take it away; it's all over the place. There is so much money in it. It's worth even more than pornog-

like Nelson, classified users into two large categories: casual (recreational) users and habitual users. It is interesting to note that the source of the sentence chosen by the newspaper is a prostitute in the Bronx who "smokes crack every day," surely a habitual user according to Nelson or Bush's classification.

Rabbit's analogy comparing Nelson to Hitler is also remarkable. The reasoning is if Nelson is a recreational user then Hitler must have been a recreational killer. Rabbit is startled by his own analogy. He can't understand why he thought of Hitler. He thinks the explanation is that his son's mustache reminded him of Hitler. Given, however, the way Rabbit's mind operates, the reader knows better.

First, we know that the commemoration of the fiftieth anniversary of the invasion of Poland by the Germans which started World War II is not far away—a piece of news which Rabbit will hear Peter Jennings, Tom Brokaw, and Dan Rather report on television. It is one more example of the many time referents that organize the chronology of *Rabbit at Rest*.

Second, a quick look at the newspaper will tell us that throughout the week Rabbit's mind has been bombarded by news of America's now ancient enemy Adolph Hitler, with neo-Nazis celebrating the centennial of the "Führer's" birthday. In effect, the *New York Times* edition of April 20, 1989, less than a week before Rabbit's analogy was produced, reminds us that "Adolph Hitler was born one hundred years ago" and goes on to analyze the fearful hopes of West Germans that nothing violent will mark the day. Not surprisingly, Hitler was on the national television evening news six times during the month of April 1989, which coincidentally is also the number of times he is mentioned in the novel. CBS carried a three-minute report on April 17 discussing, along with Hitler's coming one hundredth birthday, the growth of neo-Nazism in Germany and calling attention to the victory of right wing parties in local German elections. On April 18, Hitler was again remembered on CBS and NBC, this time because Oliver North was compared to Adolph Hitler by prosecutor John Keker in a good example of one historical text writing itself into another—past history writing itself into present history. And because Hitler's birthday celebrations happened not only in Europe but also in the United States, especially in Hayden Lake, Idaho, where neo-Nazi skinheads had their own gathering, Rabbit had another opportunity to see Hitler on television on April 22, two days after the actual birthday. Being aware of what nourished Rabbit's mind during those days brings into the interpretation much more than a possible similarity between Nelson's and Hitler's mustaches. Just as prosecutor John Keker did not compare Oliver North to Hitler by making the mustache the term of comparison, Rabbit thinks of Hitler because of his presence and significance to that particular moment of his life, probably as a synonym for evil or as an emblem of an enemy which has been brought back to life and has to be engaged.

Thus the historically-minded reader writes the text differently from Updike's narrator, although it is impossible to know to what extent the narrator, with all his awareness of time and place, is pulling the reader's leg. It is evident, however, that history writes itself into story as much as story writes itself into history. Or, put differently, one may ask if it was Hitler's anniversary which made Rabbit look at Nelson's mustache and think of Hitler, or if it was Nelson's mustache which, because of Hitler's presence in the media, made Rabbit think of him as Hitler. Whatever our answer, we have evidence enough of the impossibility of Updike's text escaping the prison house of history.

It also should be recalled that the drug problem was raised to an unprecedented level of visibility during the last year of the decade, becoming one of the most expensive governmental programs. Not only was it considered the most important domestic issue, but according to a CBS poll, it became the most important international issue, surpassing terrorism and arms control for almost 50 percent of the respondents. Certainly aware of this national concern, Bush addressed the nation during prime time on September 5, 1989, to announce what came to be known as the war on drugs plan. He denounced drugs as "the gravest domestic threat to our nation" (502) and called for a united America to fight a war on all fronts.

Waltraud Queiser Morales claims that during those days the war on drugs plan became America's new national security doctrine,[11] accompanied as it were by a "conscious effort by the government to convince the American public and the United States Congress of the intimate linkage between drug traffickers and leftist guerrillas" (155). According to Morales, the war on drugs in 1988 and 1989 can be read as a natural consequence of major foreign policy setbacks in Latin America. Considering that many parts of the plan remain classified information, this interpretation might well have been the case. Indications are that the extraordinary relevance given this issue by a president in his first major address to the nation was an attempt to temporarily replace lost enemies. With the Cold War over, the war on drugs could perhaps replace, even if for a short time, anticommunism. As Morales points out, "the average American citizen, whether he has accepted the official ideological linkage of drugs with terrorism as a global communist conspiracy or as a valid national security threat in its own right, is mobilized against international drug trafficking" (Morales 167). Rabbit's words, as we have seen, confirm that

---

[11] Following Bush's address to the nation, Senator Joseph R. Biden Jr. spoke on behalf of the Democratic party. He said: "We speak with great concern about the drug problem in America today, but we fail to appreciate or address it for what it really is—*the number one threat to our national security*" (508, my emphasis).

he associates drug trafficking with communists—people whom "you can never trust not to gang up on you" (310)—especially now that Gorbachev is visiting China and "that evil pockmarked Noriega" (310) refuses to leave power in Panama. Although a poor substitute for the ever-present forces of the Cold War, the drug war literally gives him a reason to worry and to get up in the morning (at least until the events in eastern Europe seal the end of the Cold War, and the war in the Persian Gulf consigns the drug effort into oblivion).

History thus finds its way into the novel through one of the major issues of the end of the eighties and produces or interferes with the actions and thoughts of the characters. The articulation of the drug issue with other topical events of the day reveals a process of metaphorical appropriation of remarkable versatility, as if at every step Rabbit did find the meaning he had been look-ing for behind the news.

Nelson's drug addiction, for example, surprises the Angstrom family, much like the arrest of Dale Berra, son of baseball hero Yogi Berra, comes as a surprise to the American nation. Dale Berra was arrested on charges of buying drugs from a drug ring. As Rabbit appropriates Yogi Berra's plight as a father who shares his difficulties, he tells Janice: "You don't understand the power of drugs . . . People who are into coke will kill their grandmother for a fix" (226). The historical and the fictional once again become in-extricably bound to each other.

Similarly, Nelson's quick cure parallels official reports of quick victories in the war on drugs. By the end of 1990, a year after the beginning of the plan, a White House report claimed that drug abuse among "occasional cocaine users" like Nelson had declined 11 percent. Secretary of Health and Human Services Louis W. Sullivan also declared that crack use among high school seniors had decreased from 4 percent in 1986 to 1.9 percent by the end of

1990. However, many people (like Rabbit) had difficulty believing in this quick miracle. Some experts considered the questionnaires, filled out by people who volunteered the information, unreliable indicators of addiction, especially because, as Democratic Senator Joseph Biden's Judiciary Committee discovered, the number of deaths related to cocaine use had actually increased by 10 percent since the beginning of the plan, and the number of so-called "hard core addicts" had gone up by 15 percent in the same period.

Whom was Rabbit to believe? As usual, his tendency is to trust established authority, but even that has lately become more difficult to do, for the authorities themselves appear confused. When he tells Janice of his surprise at the "drugless wonder" Nelson has become, Janice takes his remark as sarcasm and reminds him that "returning to your milieu is the hardest part of recovery" (400). Rabbit discovers that in the world of drug treatment not only has he become "milieu" but also "relational poison"—something to be controlled. Rabbit is willing to play along, but as he embraces his son, he feels the embrace is "showy and queer and forced, the kind of thing these TV evangelists tell you to do to one another, before they run off screen and get their secretaries to lay them" (401). In Rabbit's mind, Nelson has become former PTL minister Jim Bakker, presently on trial on twenty-four counts of fraud— another fallen authority figure. A Nelson transformed into Jim Bakker cannot be trusted. His son's behavior seems strange, "learned elsewhere and . . . has nothing to do with being an Angstrom" (401). And being an Angstrom is the only thing Rabbit believes he can still rely on to prevent the destabilizing forces which surround him from "aggravating" him to death.

# CHAPTER SEVEN

## THE FEAR OF AIDS

Those little HIVs, intricate as tiny spaceships, slithering off
onto his palm and up his wrist and arm into the sweat pores of
his armpit and burrowing into his bloodstream there.

—John Updike, *Rabbit at Rest*

The death motif in *Rabbit at Rest* is enhanced by the ominous im-
plicit and explicit presence of AIDS on every other page of the
novel. Of all the issues which make *Rabbit at Rest* a novel of the
eighties, AIDS is a major one. It occupies the minds of doctors,
politicians, administrators, businessmen, drug users and pushers,
journalists, movie actors, and common citizens like Rabbit every
hour of their days. More than just contributing to the death statistics, AIDS has a devastating influence over the sex life of the
whole country, bringing prejudice and fear of contagion into the
most basic routines of daily life.

In a country where the president himself had to take the AIDS
test it is not surprising to find as one of the first references to
death in the novel the name of Max Robinson, ABC's first national
black anchorman, who reportedly died of AIDS. Nor is it sur-

prising to find an HIV-infected person employed at the Angstrom's lot. Lyle, the lot's homosexual accountant, is terminally ill
and to Rabbit's satisfaction "worse off than [he himself]" (215).[1]

The importance of Lyle in the story lies in his significant contribution to the dramatization of one of the most pressing and ter-
rifying issues of the decade, helping to reveal in the process a
number of conflicts which the historically-minded reader, willingly or not, reads into the text. Furthermore, Lyle's close connection with Nelson brings the fear of contamination right into the
Angstroms' home and bedroom, throwing suspicion over Nelson's sexual preferences and overall health.

Lyle and Rabbit's encounter at the lot brings the axis of the
story into close proximity to the axis of history, and vice versa.
Rabbit is forced to face the AIDS issue in his own lot. He hates the
disease, not so much because it reminds him of his own imminent
death but because it destabilizes the world as he has known it.
The disease, he realizes, is no longer affecting only those who
have been contaminated by the deadly virus—it is affecting everybody. It has become the concern of Reagan and Bush, of the national health system, of gay and lesbian rights activists—it is suffused into the daily life of common citizens in general. Its perva-
siveness is so impressive that it even has penetrated the walls of
the Vatican. On December 26, 1988, the *New York Times* chose the
comments on AIDS made by Pope John Paul II during his Christmas message as its quotation of the day: "I invite everyone to take
up the tragic burden of these brethren of ours, and as I assure
them of my deep affection, I exhort scientists and researchers to
increase their efforts to find an effective treatment for this myste-

---

[1] Ronald Reagan was tested for infection with the AIDS virus in January 1987.
The impetus for the test was the blood transfusion received after he had been
shot on March 30, 1981. His doctor said he tested negative.

rious illness."[2] Although Rabbit is not in the least concerned with the suffering of the AIDS victims and is, in fact, repulsed by the homosexuality he associates with it, his fear of catching the disease has become part of his life.

The piece of news that Rabbit hears on television on Saturday evening, September 2, 1989, namely that "Reagan thought AIDS was as mild as measles until Rock Hudson died" (456), has already been absorbed as an example of ignorance.[3] Rabbit does not like Reagan's doctor going on radio and television and revealing secrets of his former president. But now that Hudson is dead and Reagan has realized how dangerous the virus in fact is, Rabbit has gone to the other extreme and sees AIDS endangering all segments of society—hospitals, jails, families, government, politics, coworkers, neighbors, friends, lovers, etc. When Lyle offers him his hand at their first, last, and only meeting, he cannot hide his fear:

> Harry takes the offered hand in a brief handshake and tries not to think of those little HIVs, intricate as tiny spaceships, slithering off onto his palm and up his wrist and arm into the sweat pores of his armpit and burrowing into his bloodstream there. He wipes his palm on the side of his jacket and hopes it looks like he's patting his pocket. (214)

Rabbit's fear is not his alone. When Nelson hired Lyle, three of the employees at the lot immediately quit their jobs for fear of

---

[2] *New York Times*, December 26, 1988.

[3] This piece of news had the following headline in the September 2, 1989, edition of the *New York Times:* "Actor's Illness Helped Reagan to Grasp AIDS, Doctor Says." As to the specific comment mentioned in the novel, Reagan's doctor said: "He accepted it like it was measles and it would go away." It should, furthermore, be noticed that Rock Hudson died on October 2, 1985, in Los Angeles, California. On that occasion, President Reagan praised Hudson's career and promised to increase AIDS research funds. CBS *Evening News* reported that Reagan's recognition was the nation's recognition of the need to "accelerate research."

contamination, despite Nelson's argument that "you [couldn't] catch [it] from casual contact" (213). The fear is general, both in the story and in history. A quick look at the papers of the time will indicate how accurately Updike brings into his fiction not only the spirit of the decade, but the actual concerns, fears, and hopes of the average citizen. For the record, national television broadcasts exhibited at least three hundred fifteen pieces of news and special reports in 1989 alone, which means over twenty-six per month and virtually one a day. Qualitatively and quantitatively these discussions and concerns convey with great fidelity the impact of the issue on the daily lives of ordinary citizens.

AIDS was discussed from all perspectives imaginable—legal, moral, religious, economic, political, social, medical, scientific— encompassing aspects such as the contaminated person's right to privacy versus the public's right to know and to protect itself; the number of years the virus could remain dormant in a contaminated person;[4] the discovery of new drugs and the consequences for humanity if a cure is not found; the international network of AIDS charlatans trying to profit from people's despair; the moral and religious controversy over advertising the use of condoms; the skyrocketing insurance premiums for people who did not allow themselves to be tested for AIDS; Reagan's expansion of Medicare, directed at allocating more funds for catastrophic sicknesses like AIDS; the problem of contaminated male prostitutes in American jails; the astonishing numbers of Africans infected by the AIDS virus, estimated at ten million people in 1987; the controversy over requirements for routine testing and the respect for

---

[4] On April 18, 1989, Benny Leone, an employee of Springer Motors, tells Rabbit: "That HIV virus can be inside you for five or ten years before you know it" (213). Historically, this sentence could not have been produced before May 31, 1989, when for the first time it was announced that the AIDS virus could remain dormant in the body for up to three years. Benny's sentence, therefore, was produced a month and a half before actual results were disclosed by the media.

basic rights of the individual; the closing of gay bathhouses and massage parlors; reports of AIDS victims breaking the law in order to get unauthorized medicine from other countries; the emotional impact of AIDS on families and friends; the problem of virus carriers who willingly and knowingly contaminate others (should they be treated as criminals?); the predicament of hemophiliacs and people in need of blood transfusions; the ostracism imposed upon AIDS victims, homosexuals or not; the growing concern that AIDS may not be, as originally thought, a disease of gays only; the effect of AIDS on the labor force, since most victims acquire the disease during the most productive years of their lives and are forced to take many days off from work; the connections between AIDS, intravenous drug users, and African Americans; the public hysteria and paranoia; the ubiquitous fear that a one-night encounter with a lover may mean certain death, as was the case for Alison Gertz, who caught AIDS from a one-night encounter with a bisexual man.[5] Most of these issues are directly present in *Rabbit at Rest*; others are submerged parts of the same iceberg, and it will take historically-minded readers to unveil them.

Rabbit's fears, then, have reason to be. While papers do advertise that casual contact is not infectious, there are examples of AIDS victims using their disease to terrorize and blackmail people, not to mention historic cases such as the Don Juan style bar owner in Key West who, to the despair of many, was reported to have the disease.[6] The piece of news, for instance, about "these guys in prison now bite the guards to give them AIDS with their saliva" (185) is as historically accurate as any of the others. It refers to the case of an inmate infected with the AIDS virus who

---

[5] On May 19, 1989, ABC's *20/20* told the story.
[6] On June 6 and 24, ABC's *20/20* aired a report called "Panic in Key West" telling this story.

was charged with attempted murder for biting a guard in 1988. His case was judged on August 30, 1989. The charge was reduced to first-degree assault, but indications were that even that charge was too severe. The court argued that "while AIDS may very well be transmitted through a human bite, there was no evidence to that effect at trial and we do not believe that is an established scientific fact."[7]

Rabbit's reaction to this matter, judging from his handshake with Lyle, would probably have been similar to that of the warden of the Limestone Correctional Facility, a state prison for men infected with the AIDS virus housing, at the time, 1252 prisoners. The *New York Times* edition of August 31, 1989, reported the warden's comments on the court's decision that, although there was no proof that the AIDS virus could be spread through bites, "to the best of my knowledge, to the best of my knowledge [*sic*], it hasn't been proven it can't." In fact, it had already been proven that AIDS could not be transmitted by saliva. Like the warden, however, Rabbit is afraid.

Similarly, Lyle's attempt to blackmail Janice also dramatizes historically-based incidents and circumstances. Lyle's illness explains, in part, why the lot's accounts are not ready when Rabbit wants them, even though, as Lyle himself puts it, the computer allows him to do in a few hours what Mildred Kroust, the former accountant of Springer Motors, would take a week to do. We learn through Benny that Mildred's office was made into a  conference

---

[7] In the *New York Times*, August 31, 1989. A similar case was reported by NBC news on December 7, 1985, when AIDS carrier John Richards, from Flint, Michigan, was arrested for spitting on officers. He was later indicted on attempted murder charges. It is also important to recall that on December 18, 1985, the Massachusetts General Hospital announced that research findings indicated that AIDS was not transmitted by saliva. The results were published in the *New England Journal of Medicine*. Thus, from a scientific perspective, Rabbit's fear of being contaminated by a handshake is unjustifiable.

room: "There is a couch in there if anybody needs all of a sudden to take a nap. Lyle used to, but now he works mostly at home, what with his illness" (213). We learn that part of the files are at Lyle's home, which confirms Benny's observation and suggests forced absences from work caused by AIDS.

Lyle's actual attempt to blackmail the Angstroms not only dramatizes middle America's and Rabbit's prejudices against gays but also brings into fiction examples of the desperation to survive which led some victims of AIDS to consider involvement in illegal activities. Lyle refuses to show the books and discs with the accounts of Springer Motors. When Janice, filled with both undeniable prejudice and good reasons, threatens to fire him, he immediately says that you cannot fire somebody with AIDS because that would be considered discrimination. [8] He is obviously making use of a safeguard which the system has already created, given the dimension of the epidemic and the remarkable demonstration of strength of organized groups. Since showing the books to his boss is his duty, Lyle appears to be a con man trying to hide his and Nelson's wrongdoing.

It is interesting to notice here how Rabbit similarly appropriates the coeval Iran-Contra scandal and brings it to bear upon the issue. In Rabbit's mind, Lyle is a potential Oliver North in the context of the present experience: "What else could Lyle have been hiding? Now they'll have the wind up so we should start moving or they'll shred everything like Ollie North" (225).

---

[8] Perhaps the most memorable AIDS antidiscrimination law was announced on October 6, 1988. As of that date, testing positive for the AIDS virus cannot be used against individuals in the work force. The antidiscrimination issue was almost as old as AIDS itself. On November 7, 1985, Tom Shuttleworth filed suit against his employer who allegedly fired him because he had AIDS. A similar case was reported on December 12, 1985, when Johnny Warner lost his job because he tested HIV-positive. Later tests showed he was HIV-negative.

Updike could have made Rabbit end his sentence without mentioning Ollie North. The text would still have meaning, and the sentence would be complete. The difference, one easily infers, would be that history would acquire a much less categorical relevance, disguising what Updike tries so patiently and carefully to make explicit. Updike's technique forces the reader to help write the text. The reference to a historical figure who is on trial at the exact moment the action in the story takes place brings to life, through the reader's memory, a universe of implications, especially the administration's honesty with the American "family" and North's connection to Reagan and Bush—the latter paralleling Lyle's connection with Nelson. It is, therefore, not surprising that the news of Bush and Reagan being subpoenaed to testify as defense witnesses for Oliver North at his conspiracy trial is made part of the story.[9] The simile, furthermore, stresses a trait of Rabbit's referred to in the introduction, namely that Rabbit's mind is strongly metaphorical in its apprehension of the world, so that the new is always filtered through the old. In other words, Lyle (the new experience) is understood as a potential Oliver North (the widely publicized and already old experience).

We should remember that North declared he had shredded pertinent documents as early as July 5, 1987. Almost two years later, on January 5, 1989, Rabbit would have had a chance to see a report on Oliver North's shredding of self-incriminatory evidence on NBC's 5:30 P.M. news and then again on CBS and NBC on April 12. On April 13, he admitted on all the major television networks to falsifying records. Oliver North's trial continued

---

[9] Ronald Reagan and George Bush were subpoenaed on December 30, 1988. On April 7, 1989, *The New York Times* reports that "the judge in the trial of Oliver North rejected an attempt to force Ronald Reagan to appear as a witness, declaring that no written evidence suggested that Mr. Reagan authorized acts for which Mr. North was being tried."

throughout 1989, with many witnesses testifying for and against North during the months of March and April.[10]

Rabbit also appropriates the imminent certainty of death brought about by AIDS in a curious way. Seemingly out of the blue Rabbit and Lyle, two strangers until that moment, engage in a lengthy conversation about the real prospect of death, "the actual taste of [which Rabbit has] in [his] mouth" (218). Rabbit feels free to start this conversation because he believes he and Lyle somehow share the same basic predicament: both will soon be dead. Rabbit's realization that Lyle is only about half his age makes him travel once more down memory lane. He realizes that at Lyle's age he "was setting type the old-fashioned way, and dreaming about ass" (219). He remembers Thelma and their unexpected sexual encounter in the Caribbean during the seventies when they had anal sex. His experience is read directly into Lyle's homosexuality and then back into his own experience: "Ass, one way or another, does us in: membrane too thin, those little HIVs sneak right through . . . being queer isn't all roses" (219).

Reagan's attitudes toward AIDS and gays are also presented with remarkable generative power. During the discussion with Harry, Lyle throws all his indignation at Reagan: "They're developing new drugs. All the time. The French. The Chinese. Trichosanthin. TIBO derivatives. Eventually the FDA will have to let them in, even if they are a bunch of Reaganite fascist homophobes who wouldn't mind seeing us all dead" (218). This dialogue takes place on April 18, 1989. On April 10, the Food and Drug Administration (FDA) had denied IMREG permission to sell a drug it claimed was effective. Instead the FDA ordered the company to

---

[10] North's trial was in the national evening television news thirty-three times during March and fifty times during April. When the Pennsylvania section of *Rabbit at Rest* begins on April 10, Oliver North is on his third day of testimony in

retest the experimental drug. It is also important to register that by June 13 the *New York Times* reports that indeed "AZT is now the only drug licensed in the United States for treating Acquired Immunodeficiency Syndrome."[11] The article, written by Lawrence K. Altman, makes reference to two experimental drugs, Dideoxynosine and Dideooxycytidine. These drugs were presented as novelties at the international AIDS meeting in Montreal in June 1989, six years after the discovery of the virus. The drugs to which Lyle makes reference are, therefore, probably part of the smuggling scheme which the harsh restrictions of the FDA seem to have stimulated. On April 18, the *New York Times* reported on a root-derived drug against AIDS. In retrospect, one cannot help inferring that the FDA's restrictions had good technical reasons to exist, for none of the clandestine drugs seem to have shown major results to this day. But as Janice later points out, because the experimental drugs had to be smuggled into the country, their costs were extremely high. This, in part, explains the origin of Springer Motors' debt. Even victims who used only the legalized AZT would spend, according to estimates, a minimum of $8000 per year.

A few days before the April 18 dialogue between Rabbit and Lyle, AIDS drugs were in the news throughout the country, with ABC's evening news presenting a five-minute report on the subject. A large number of untested remedies were discussed, including spiritual healing and typhoid vaccine. On the occasion Martin Delany, an AIDS support group leader, claimed that "a cornucopia of crap" was being sold by people unscrupulous enough to profit from other people's despair.

---

his Iran-Contra trial. The trial ended on May 4, with North convicted on three of twelve counts.

[11] *New York Times*, June 13, 1989.

A similar report on drugs was aired on April 13, 1989, on the CBS *Evening News*, referring specifically to a new AIDS drug, compound Q, developed in China. The miracle drug was reportedly found in cucumber root. A similar report was aired by NBC on April 27, a few days after the April 18 dialogue. Lyle's reference to the Chinese shows once again that the words he pronounces are not the product of Updike's fantasies but of his conscious and determined effort to recreate a believable, historically-situated individual.

Lyle's condemnation of the Reagan administration finds its justification in the angry criticism of gay and lesbian activists, medical doctors, and university professors who criticized not only the supposedly weak effort being made by the government to support AIDS victims legally and financially, but also the vagueness and lack of aggressiveness of its educational campaign. These protests gained strength in October 1988. In one of these protests in Rockville, Maryland, protesters went as far as burning an effigy of President Reagan. More than that, however, Lyle's harsh criticism brings to the text a well-known political conflict between conservatives and liberals over ideas of traditional marriage and alternative sexual preferences. Whereas conservatives like Wally George were preaching throughout America that God "made Adam and Eve and not Adam and Steve" and would certainly not "mind to see all [homosexuals] dead" and were announcing that AIDS was a disease of sinners, liberal groups tended to tolerate (if not exactly endorse) alternative lifestyles and affirm that AIDS was not an exclusively homosexual disease. Family values and sexual habits inherited from previous decades were being placed in check. On April 11, 1989, for instance, NBC had a two-minute report on a government survey directed at studying the sexual habits of the American population to better understand the spread of the virus. This probably explains why

Updike has Pru (unlike Rabbit) suggest that promiscuity and needle sharing, not homosexuality, may be the major causes for the
alarming diffusion of the disease.

Lyle's direct attack on the FDA for its restrictions on the use of
certain drugs has a visible historical counterpart. As early as February 1989, protesters demonstrated in various places in the
country against the FDA policies on drug approval. On one such
occasion, after three years of testing, the FDA finally approved the
use of aerosol pentamidine, a drug said to prevent pneumonia
and other AIDS-related diseases.

Since the 1980s was the decade of the AIDS epidemic, it is only
natural to expect that it would serve as an action-generating factor
in a story as scene-centered as Rabbit's. Immersed in the world of
AIDS, the major characters of *Rabbit at Rest* have their whole lives
affected by it: Pru refuses to have sex with Nelson; Rabbit is afraid
of making love with Thelma, after ten years of their secret love
affair; and Rabbit now sees the actualization of sex as a "willing
slide into death" (202). Although he is ashamed to tell Thelma his
fears about AIDS—"it would be spitting in her wide-open face"
(203)—he finally confesses that he is afraid of "Ronnie's little
bugs" (207). Even Thelma has to concede that "we must all be
more careful" (207) and tells him during their last encounter:
"You be careful. Keep brushing your teeth, and I'll brush mine"
(207). [12]

Aware of the same danger and unwilling to risk her life, Pru
conscientiously has a condom handy when having sex with Rabbit and only has sex with her husband again when he proves to

---

[12] Rabbit's fear could be said to have been strongly influenced by Rock Hudson's
lover Marc Christian, who in February 1989 was awarded millions in compen-
satory damages because Hudson failed to tell him he had AIDS, causing him to
contract the deadly virus.

her that he is HIV-negative.[13] To have sex without these precautions would be suicidal. As Pru puts it, "Why should I risk my life sleeping with you, you addict, you think I want to get AIDS from your dirty needles when you're speedballing or from some cheap coke whore you screw when you're gone until two in the morning?" (160).[14] In her refusal to sleep with Nelson, Pru voices one of the major concerns of authorities—the transmission of the AIDS virus through the collective use of contaminated needles by drug users. To a large extent, the war against drugs was also a war against AIDS, as shown in numerous documentaries and television segments of the 1980s.

One can better appreciate how much AIDS makes *Rabbit at Rest* a book of the eighties when one remembers how absent these fears were in books of the 1960s such as *Couples* and *Rabbit Redux*, or in *Rabbit Is Rich*, a book of the 1970s. One can also appreciate history's contribution to the novel's making when one is aware that there was hardly a day during the second half of 1989 in which AIDS did not produce major reports in the *New York Times* and in the media in general.[15] The fear of death was everywhere and with every individual. With Americans from different walks of life in its cast of characters, *Rabbit at Rest* could not fail to register some of the ways in which the AIDS experience was perceived. It is an invitation to the reader to value the historical memorabilia which, like pearls, are scattered throughout the novel.

---

[13] In his interview with Don Williams, Updike commented: "AIDS strikes me as terribly sad and a lot of clutter around what should be a rather pure act."

[14] In Tacoma, Washington, one man named David Purchase decided to do something about the spread of AIDS—distribute clean needles to intravenous drug users. The story was aired on ABC news on February 8, 1989.

[15] On Sunday, June 18, 1989, AIDS experts told Mayor Koch that "they opposed the New York City's Health Commissioner's call for mandatory tracing of people who had sex or shared needles with victims."

As happens with Updike's tetralogy as a whole and with his other novels, *Rabbit at Rest* uncovers the tip of an enormous historical iceberg while dramatizing the lives of ordinary people. It suggests and reveals the generating power of the underlying and never fully recoverable scene, showing that AIDS is part of a whole set of circumstances and events which threatens to destabilize the world as it is and which Rabbit would like to preserve. It is not the fear of physical death of individuals which ultimately worries Rabbit, but the fear that AIDS is one more indication that the soul and the heart of America are sick and that things are falling apart.

# CHAPTER EIGHT

## A FEW MORE INTIMATIONS

I loved Shillington not as one loves Capri or New York, because they are special, but as one loves one's own body and consciousness, because they are synonymous with being.

—John Updike, *Self-Consciousness*

The sense of death which pervades *Rabbit at Rest* also manifests itself in Rabbit's appropriation of a multitude of events and personalities of the world of sports. He is selectively interested in the lives of individuals which tell him something about his own life, as it was and as it is. His attention focuses especially on football and baseball player Deion Sanders; on baseball player Mike Schmidt; on former baseball star Pete Rose, now manager of the Cincinnati Reds; on Bartlet Giamatti, scholar and baseball executive; on baseball players Steve Bedrosian and Juan Samuel; and on tennis players Ivan Lendl and Martina Navratilova. As usual, although Rabbit is very concerned with how the world works, he is by far more concerned with what it means, and all these sports heroes seem to tell him something about it.

In Part I of the novel, football and baseball player Deion Sanders is a constant presence. Sanders's immoderate and irreverent behavior rings a bell with Rabbit, not so much with what Rabbit is now but with what he once was. Sanders, who calls himself "Prime Time," very openly expresses his goal in life: "I always wanted to be No. 1 . . . I always want to be the star of the show."[1] Readers familiar with *Rabbit, Run* will immediately find the source of this identification. Rabbit, too, was number one in his community for a few years, and he imagined that the quality of his basketball could be transferred to the quality of his life. When he realizes that his life with Janice is second-rate, he runs. His confession to his Jewish friends that his interest in Sanders is personal—that he, too, "had a little taste of it once. Athletics. Everybody cheering, loving you. Wanting a piece" (58)—should come as no surprise. It confirms that Updike has his character choose out of the world of events those which somehow bear a relationship to the experience and behavior of his hero. The justification of Sanders's frequent appearances in the novel is not to be found only in the remarkable media coverage he receives but more so in what his way of being has to contribute towards the development of Rabbit's story—a story which in the eighties finds its energy in a desperate need to match the desire to be alive with the ever-present memory of a life already lived. Through Sanders, Rabbit vicariously re-experiences an important fragment of his personal trajectory.

Part II of the novel opens in Pennsylvania in early April, the cruelest month for death-conscious Rabbit, for Brewer is a pool of memory and desire. He likes to be back in his hometown at this time of year because of spring's "secret sap that runs through everybody's lives" (181) and because he takes some masochistic pleasure in "freshening his memory and hurting himself with the pieces of his old self that cling to almost every corner of the

---

[1] *Atlanta Constitution*, December 26, 1988.

Brewer area" (181), like "dull roots" in need of being stirred back to life.

He also likes to be back in Pennsylvania because by this time "baseball has come north" (181). His hero right now is Mike Schmidt—"Schmidt [who] this year [has hit] two home runs in the first two games, *squelching all talk that he was through*" (181, my emphasis). Mike Schmidt is mentioned again and again throughout the novel.

The choice of Schmidt as his hero in *Rabbit at Rest* reminds us of *Rabbit Is Rich*, in which he also cannot accept that he is "running out of gas" despite what the world is saying. Just as he wishes to postpone his own death, he wishes to postpone Schmidt's. And apparently he has good reason to believe that Schmidt can postpone his professional "death" in baseball. On Tuesday afternoon, April 18, 1989, the veteran's success story is reported in the *New York Times*:

> Mike Schmidt's three-run homer capped a seven-run fourth inning for Philadelphia. Schmidt's homer off Jeff Pico, a reliever, was his second in two days and the 54th of his career. It also was his 78th home run against the Cubs and his 50th in Wrigley Field.[2]

The piece of news that Rabbit hears on the radio that same afternoon is even richer in detail and deserves to be quoted in full for purposes of comparison. It effectively shows how Rabbit lets history invade his life, and how his mind wanders from April 18, 1989, to 1950 and then back again to the present:

> On the radio on the way home, he hears that Mike Schmidt, who exactly two years ago, on April 18, 1987, slugged his five hundredth home run, against the Pittsburgh Pirates in Three River Stadium, is closing in on Richie Ashburn's total of 2,217 hits to become the hittingest Phillie ever.

---

[2] The *New York Times*, April 6, 1989.

Rabbit remembers Ashburn. One of the Whiz Kids who beat the Dodgers
for the pennant the fall Rabbit became a high-school senior. Curt Sim-
mons, Del Ennis, Dick Sisler in center, Stan Lopata behind the plate. Beat
the Dodgers the last game of the season, then lost to the Yankees four
straight. In 1950 he was seventeen and had led the county B league with
817 points his junior season. Remembering these statistics helps settle his
agitated mood, stirred up by seeing Thelma and Lyle, a mood of stirred-
up unsatisfied desire at whose fringes licks the depressing idea that
nothing matters very much, we'll all soon be dead. (220)

As can be noted, Rabbit's agitated mood settles when he remembers his success in the fifties, but the idea that he, like everybody else, will "soon be dead" depresses him greatly. The memory of what he once was, added to the realization of the inevitability of death, creates an unbearable combination. We should recall at this point that Rabbit is returning from the Springer Motors
lot where he has just discovered that Nelson "has taken down the
old blown-up photos of Harry in his glory days as a basketball
star, with the headlines calling him Rabbit" (208). In other words,
he has just realized that he has been discarded; that his personal
history, the memory of himself, has been erased; and that in one
sense he is already dead. The looked-for meaning behind the
news of veteran Mike Schmidt, therefore, seems to be that no
matter how much Rabbit cheers for him, he will (on a larger scale)
follow everybody's journey toward oblivion and death. He, like
Rabbit, will soon be erased despite his stardom.

On the next day, April 19, 1989, Rabbit again hears news of
Schmidt, who played the night before in a game between the
Phillies and the Mets—a game which we are told Rabbit watched.
This time he is with Charlie, the old friend he so much admires
for his capacity to interpret "the big picture" (232). Somehow
Rabbit "has never gotten over the idea that the news is going to
mean something to him" (232). The news is not just an event, an
object with an independent existence, something which can sub-

sist separate from himself, unaware of him. Pieces of news are facts which are "like the individual letters, with their spikes and loops and thorns, that make up words" (*SC* 2). They have a meaning, even when we don't like it.  As he mentions Schmidt's feat, Charlie gives him the cruel meaning: "Schmidt'll wilt. He's old" (232). Having had his "admiration for Schmidt checked" (233), Rabbit realizes that "you can't live through these athletes, they don't know you exist" (233).

And that is precisely what Rabbit has been trying to do, vicariously live his present life through successful athletes—in this case, the famous baseball player—nourishing the fantasy that Schmidt knows of his existence and cares for him. Charlie denies him this pleasure and throws him back to discussing the crude reality of the latest deaths and catastrophes; namely, the explosion of the PanAm aircraft, the soccer fans at an English stadium being crushed to death, and the recent explosion on the battleship *Iowa*.

As Charlie predicted, veteran Mike Schmidt's glory did not last long. After a serious injury to his right shoulder, Schmidt tried to return to baseball. Reports are that he played well for a week, but after seeing that his spectacular skills had vanished, he decided to retire. "I look at the Will Clarks and the Kevin Mitchels," Schmidt said, "and I see the player I used to be . . . It hurts to know that I'm no longer that player" (Sloan 163). Rabbit, who on every other page of the novel is reminded of his own withering strength and skills, shares Schmidt's psychological pain. In some ways, he is indeed like Schmidt. By June, Schmidt had retired, and Rabbit, having involuntarily retired from the lot, thinks Schmidt did the right thing: "Schmidt did what Pete Rose was too dumb to: quit, when you've had it. Take your medicine, don't prolong the agony with all these lawyers" (356).[3]

---

[3] Mike Schmidt retired on May 29, 1989, at age thirty-nine.

"These lawyers" are for veteran baseball player Pete Rose what the medical doctors are for Rabbit, the veteran small-town basketball star of the fifties: the only possible salvation. Pete Rose, a national role model who neither smoked nor drank, a hero of two generations of fans, was now being accused of involvement with drugs, tax evasion, and (worst of all) placing bets on his own team. His survival in the world of baseball depended exclusively on his lawyers' ability to defend him from various charges. Throughout 1988 and 1989, his lawyers tried desperately to prove his innocence. Eventually, he was banned from baseball for life. The news made the front page of the *New York Times* on two consecutive days—August 24 and 25, 1989, and was in all the major American newspapers and national television news broadcasts during those days.

The actual importance of Pete Rose for the average American may be measured by his constant presence on the national television networks during this period. From April to September 1989, for example, Rose was on the CBS, ABC, and NBC evening news broadcasts seventy times. No wonder that by August Rabbit grows tired of the news and declares himself "sick of hearing about [Pete Rose]" (384). Rose, however, remains a constant but waning presence in the media until the end of the year.

Rabbit appropriates Pete Rose's experience with ambiguity, reflecting the ambiguous feelings of the country. Although he becomes more and more disappointed by what is revealed about Rose's past activities (by August it had been widely publicized, though not categorically determined, that he had participated in illegal gambling and had been involved with drugs at the beginning of the decade), he somehow thinks it is not right that a public figure should have his survival depend so much on "hustle" and "grit." Rabbit, who had always admired Rose's feats, gradually has to accept the hard evidence that maybe his hero did not play for "pure joy," as he and so many others had imagined. He still thinks Rose, despite everything that is being said against him, deserves to be included in the Hall of Fame, given his remarkable career achievements. Rabbit's attitude is similar to a well-known placard carried by one of Rose's fans in those days: FREE MR. BASEBALL, FREE PETE ROSE! GIVE THE KIDS A HERO! In an America plagued by drugs, AIDS, debt, foreigners, and lack of discipline, Rose's disgrace is unbearably iconoclastic for a nationalist like Rabbit. Yet despite his respect for Rose, Schmidt's way of retiring is "[his] idea of a classy ballplayer" (419). His preference for Mike Schmidt's quick retirement over Pete Rose's endless and painful struggle to survive despite his "advanced" age is not only a more adequate explanation for his own resistant early retirement from the lot, but it also supports his gradual acceptance of the inevitability of death.

Bart Giamatti is also very conveniently present in the news during Rabbit's journey south. The former president of Yale University, teacher of English and comparative literature, baseball commissioner, and president of the National Baseball League (who had a few days earlier declared Pete Rose ineligible for life) died of a massive heart attack on Friday, September 1. Described by the CBS *Evening News* as a man who always showed "grace under pressure" and who considered "academia his brain [and] baseball his soul," Giamatti died at the age of fifty-one at his summer house in Edgartown, Massachusetts.

Rabbit's first reaction is to attribute Giamatti's death to Pete Rose's curse—Pete Rose, whom he feels an urge to protect, now that he has also been "banned" from home. With his usual metaphorical form of appropriation at work, he realizes that Giamatti is, after all, much like himself:

*Only fifty-one*, Rabbit thinks. Police took Giamatti to the Martha's Vine-
yard Hospital where he was worked upon for an hour and a half; the
emergency team several times succeeded in restoring the electric mechanism of the heartbeat, but Giamatti was at last pronounced dead. That little electric twitch: without it we're so much rotting meat. One of the first
things he ought to do in Florida is make an appointment with Dr. Morris
. . . He was a heavy man and a heavy smoker. *At least I'm no smoker.* (447)

There is a lot of reporting in this stretch of discourse, all of it
matching the historic record precisely, but there is certainly more
slant involved in the reporting than Updike wants us to believe
from the sentences and phrases in italics. Giamatti's age, his pas-
sion for sports, the nature of his illness, the circumstances surrounding his death—all these are details which clearly bring
Giamatti closer to Rabbit, making the process of appropriation a
natural consequence. Giamatti's sudden death becomes more than
a reminder that he has to see the doctor as soon as he arrives in
Florida. It prefigures  what is about to happen to him, where,
when, how, and why.

Although Rabbit does not have the scholarly erudition of Giamatti, he certainly (like so many middle Americans) shares Giamatti's enthusiasm for baseball. The tone of Rabbit's description
of his infatuation with spring and the way he associates the arrival of the season of new life with the arrival of baseball could very
well have come out of Giamatti's pen. About this psychological
association Giamatti writes:

It breaks your heart. It is designed to break your heart. The game begins
in the spring, when everything else begins again, and it blossoms in the
summer, filling the afternoons and evenings, and then as soon as the chill
rains come, it stops and leaves you to face the fall alone. You count on it,
you rely on it to buffer the passage of time, to keep the memory of sunshine and high skies alive and then, just when the days are twilight,
when you need it most, it stops. (Sloan 453)

It is easy to see Rabbit's appropriation of Giamatti's experience when we observe the other similarities between the two men. Rabbit, too, will soon be at his summer house; he, too, is overweight; he, too, has heart problems; he, too, is over fifty; and he, too, is a lover of baseball. With so many similarities, all Rabbit can do is try to find a differentiating factor: "At least I'm no smoker," he concludes, hoping this may save him from losing that "electric twitch" which protects him and all human beings from becoming "rotting meat."

By mid-June when his baseball team shows its worst record in history and trades away two of its "old all-stars," Steve Bedrosian and Juan Samuel, Rabbit "devours" the event and concludes that "there's no such thing as loyalty any more" (350). With Mike Schmidt retired and with Nelson having removed his pictures from the walls at the lot, Rabbit feels that the lights of his "stardom" are dwindling, just like Bedrosian's and Samuel's. Not even the month-long success of the Phillies following the trade of their famous players manages to interest Rabbit again. His identification is with the older players who are no longer there. These new ones somehow do not exist for him, for he cannot see in them anything significant which could make it worth the effort of bringing them into his life.

In sports, the older generation faced more defeats before Rabbit's last heart attack: Ivan Lendl, the great tennis player, was defeated in the U.S. Open tennis championship by the younger German Boris Becker, only one day after Martina Navratilova was defeated by the also young and German Steffi Graf. As Rabbit watches twenty-four-year-old Becker defeat Lendl, "he gets depressed . . . Lendl seemed old and tired and stringy, though he's only twenty-eight" (470). His feeling had been very similar a few days earlier when he watched tennis player Chris Evert play her last professional tennis match. At age thirty-four, Evert claimed that she was losing her concentration and thought she was too old for tennis: "She packed it in too. There comes a time" (488). Age-conscious and color-conscious Rabbit notes that Evert lost to a player who was young and black.

It seems to Rabbit that things are out of place, that the young and now the blacks are telling him how the world should be run. Like Mike Schmidt, Pete Rose, Ivan Lendl, Martina Navratilova, and Chris Evert, it is time for retiring, to call it quits. And perhaps it is time for dying, like Giamatti, like Roy Orbison, like Max Robinson, like Thelma, like so many others.

To make matters worse, African Americans seemed to be taking over the country in other spheres as well. In New York, the black Democratic candidate David N. Dinkins enjoyed a sweeping victory over white three-term mayor Edward I. Koch, becoming the first black mayor in New York history. And finally, as if the decisive blow, for the third time in American history a black Miss America was elected—all during the last two weeks of the story.[4]

The weight carried by these events seems too much for his typically American heart to take. The meaning behind the news seems to be that his old, stable, white world is eroding. And because it is time to reclaim his territory lost to blacks in all major cities, he puts on his tennis shoes and ventures downtown and into "forbidden" territory: "After all, is it a free country or not?" (490). Emblematically, he chooses black Tiger to be his adversary in a one-on-one basketball game. With winner-take-nothing irony, the game is won by Rabbit, but his excessive effort causes him to suffer a fulminating heart attack and ultimately lose his life. His

---

[4] On September 16, 1989, Debbye Turner, a veterinary student, was crowned Miss America. A *Chicago Defender* poll concludes that "Debbye Turner's crowning as the nation's third black Miss America will not change the negative views some whites have about blacks" (September 16, 1989).

sense of triumph on his deathbed, however, seems to come less from a pleasure derived from a victory in the world of sports than from a final affirmation of white predominance in the social realm: "He thinks of telling her about Tiger and *I won* but the impulse passes" (511).

# CONCLUSION

Brewer and all the world are just frills on himself, like the lace
around a plump satin valentine, himself the heart of the universe, like the Dalai Lama.

—John Updike, *Rabbit at Rest*

As in the previous Rabbit novels, the Rabbit of *Rabbit at Rest* is the
epitome of middle America. He not only lives *in* a particular time
and place, he lives *through* it or *because of* it, appropriating the
American scene in all its complexity and polyphony, from major
political, social, and economic events to the cultural memorabilia
as expressed in songs, films, television shows, television adver-
tisements, cars, and sports. All of these participate in the development of the thoughts and actions of the characters, becoming
inseparable from the story being told.

The mind frame with which Rabbit approaches these events is
essentially metaphoric. He views historical manifestations in
terms of the values he brings with him from earlier decades; present history, in all of its manifold forms of expression, exists only
as it exists for him, holds meaning for him, and can be applied to
practical day-to-day life by him. The historical moment insinuates
itself into Rabbit's life at all times, following a remarkable month-

to-month, week-to-week, and even day-to-day synchrony, so much so that his thoughts and actions are always motivated by an appropriation of a specific historical moment. The same may be said of the other important characters in Updike's novel.

As time passes and new historical experiences are appropriated, a process of "cannibalization" sets in, quite literally translating these experiences into the characters' lives. As scenic dislocations occur, leading the characters into worlds of enormous variety and complexity, experiences define and redefine themselves, with the factual materiality of events and circumstances becoming the motive for conflicts and interactions.

Thus it happens that, in December 1988, for example, Rabbit's wife Janice sees the movie *Working Girl* and, having "devoured" this experience, starts thinking and acting to become what the title suggests. The world of *Working Girl* will be with her and Rabbit throughout the novel, for in the metaphoric way of apprehending the world, she has *become* the character that Melanie Griffith played in the movie. Rabbit, similarly, having seen on television the movie *The Return of Martin Guerre* with Gerard Depardieu, *becomes* in many respects the man who usurps another man's identity and ultimately his wife.

Rabbit's interest in Florida State University football player Deion Sanders follows a similar criterion of selection: identification with some aspect of the other's life. His interest not only shows the metaphorical trope at work but also invites the reader to recall what happened during the *Rabbit, Run* days when, after having a little taste of fame, he finds it unbearable to live a second-rate life and decides to run. Sanders is, thus, a historical device of the present brought into the story to revive the smothered hero who inhabits Rabbit's past.

Rabbit's mind brings into his life experiences of all kinds, ranging from an old Doris Day movie of which a specific kind of pajamas may remind him, to the fog which dims everyone's vision during the football game between the Chicago Bears and the Philadelphia Eagles and is remembered as Rabbit lies in the hospital and thinks of himself as being "in a fog" (178), to pieces of news of highly localized interest. In Florida, for example, he reads in the *Fort Myers News-Press* about this "guy convicted of picking up a twelve-year-old girl and getting her to smoke dope and raping her and then burning her alive somehow and now complaining about the cockroaches and rats in the cell on death row and telling the reporter, 'I've always tried to do the best I can, but I'm no angel. And I'm no killer either.' His saying this made Harry laugh, it rang a kind of bell with him. No angel yet no killer" (9). Readers familiar with *Rabbit Redux* will immediately remember why Rabbit thinks he, in some ways, is like this convict. He also took drugs in the sixties with a teenager; he also had sex with a girl young enough to be his daughter; he also saw her die when his home caught fire; he also is no angel yet no killer; he also tries to do his best; and with his arteries clogged and so many people around him dying, he also is on a death row of sorts. In this case, not much effort is necessary for Rabbit's metaphoric mind to bring the outside world into familiarity.

As Rabbit's problems with Nelson's drug addiction increase, he thinks his situation is exactly like that of former baseball star Yogi Berra. Both have sons addicted to cocaine, and Berra's plight becomes his plight. If we consider that Berra's son was arrested on April 20 and that Janice and Rabbit's conversation in *Rabbit at Rest* takes place on April 18, one has the impression that "fiction" becomes "reality." Yet it is clear that the intrusion of a "fact-to-be" is a pleasant, probably deliberate, "mistake" made by Updike, given the proximity and pertinence of the concern. Technically, Rabbit could not have identified with the problem before the problem existed, yet (like himself) Berra may have suspected his son's involvement with drugs before the fact became public.

April brings other news into Rabbit's life, sometimes in indirect or seemingly trivial ways. On April 18, for example, Rabbit thinks of his mother-in-law, who, we are told, died the day after Prince William was born (June 22, 1982). He goes on to tell us that two things had interested her to her last day: the future of the British monarchy and the John Hinckley trial. A look at the historical records, however, suggests that these two concerns are more likely Rabbit's or the narrator's than they were his mother-in-law's. Since Prince William was born in June, it is unlikely that Rabbit indeed thinks of his mother-in-law and then of Hinckley and Princess Diana and her son. Knowing how much Rabbit's mind is stimulated by the heat of the historical moment, the reader tends to think the opposite is the case. The evidence to support this scene-centered reading is that, as usual, Rabbit thinks what he thinks when he thinks it (that is, in April) because the publicized events make him do so. John Hinckley, it should be recalled, was about to give his first public testimony since trying to assassinate President Reagan. Hinckley's appearance on national television on April 20 was preceded by a strong presence in the media. Rabbit, it seems, thinks of his mother-in-law because Hinckley is in the news and not because he gratuitously remembers the day she died. Similarly, Rabbit's reference to the future of the British monarchy, more specifically to Prince Williams's birth two months in advance, probably finds its origin in the constant presence of Princess Diana on all national television networks during those same days. Princess Diana was shown on television visiting hospitals and comforting victims of the Sheffield soccer stadium accident, also mentioned in the novel.

The recovery of such historical trivia, unimportant as it may seem, shows an unusually circuitous form of appropriation that reveals how subtle, intricate, and complex Updike's knitting together of history and fiction can be. These references are not meant as direct metaphors but are a means of adding strength to the ubiquitous presence of death in the novel via a thin thread of interconnections. Careful observation will show that Rabbit's train of thought follows this path: Rabbit thinks of Hinckley and of Princess Diana because he sees them on television and in the papers, which in turn leads him to think of his mother-in-law, then of her illness (diabetes), then of her fears of having her legs amputated like her mother did, which makes him remember late Hannah Koerner (whose legs were amputated), which leads him to the conclusion of his reasoning—"hard to believe he will ever be as dead as Hannah Koerner" (191). History is appropriated here in a wonderfully indirect way through the memories it allows Rabbit to construe and make meaningful to his life in the present. The essence of the metaphoric trope, therefore, continues to predominate.

The April 19 explosion on the battleship *Iowa* is also appropriated by the characters in a curious way. Rabbit finds it strange that it happened "for no apparent reason" (233), to which his friend Charlie replies, "Everything has some little tiny reason, even when we can't see it. A little spark somewhere, a little crack in the metal" (233). Charlie's metonymical mind attributes this and other accidents simply to the large quantity of people living on the planet. The world, in his view, has become "jammed," so overcrowded that accidents are bound to happen. Charlie's observation is immediately translated by the narrator into Rabbit's world of metaphor, and it becomes part of his own personal experience:

> Rabbit's heart dips, thinking that from Nelson's point of view *he himself is a big part of the crowding* [my emphasis]. That time he screamed outside the burning house at 26 Vista Crescent, *I'll kill you.* He didn't mean it. A

spark, a crack in metal. A tiny flaw. When you die you do the world a favor. (233)

It is Charlie's version of the recent accidents, or his suggestion
of how we should think about these events, that finally is appropriated by Rabbit. He metaphorically becomes part of the crowd
and feels partially responsible for the overcrowding. As a consequence, the fate of the victims will eventually be his.

At the end of April, after being bombarded by a full week of
national television news about Adolph Hitler's one hundredth
birthday, during a discussion involving the Angstrom family's
crisis due to Nelson's drug addiction Rabbit hears his son's definition of himself as a recreational user of drugs and responds,
"like Hitler was a recreational killer" (260). Rabbit wonders why
he said what he said and thinks it is his son's mustache that
makes him recall Hitler. Having acted upon his own inference
and judgment and having transformed it into fact, he suggests
that "if the kid would just shave [his mustache] off . . . he maybe
could feel some compassion, and they could make a fresh start"
(260). The metaphor compares his son to Hitler, but the significance of the experience is revealed through the verbalization of
Rabbit's own anxiety. Although its origin lies in the late forties,
the reader knows that it is the historical commemorations of the
eighties (not the mustache) which bring the metaphor to mind.
Ultimately, what Rabbit sees in Nelson's brutal attack on his wife
Pru is the materialization of America's old enemy, brought right
into his home by the media through the events of the present.

In May, the Dalai Lama is back in the news, the S and L scandal continues, the Chinese students have taken Tiananmen
Square, Manuel Noriega refuses to leave power in Panama, and
President George Bush and the first lady are reported to be taking
showers with their dog Millie. In each of these news items (some

of them already discussed at length) Rabbit finds some relevance to his life.

Rabbit has identified with the Dalai Lama since 1959, when the Buddhist leader escaped the communist Chinese forces invading Tibet. In those days, readers familiar with *Rabbit, Run* will recall that Rabbit was escaping from what he considered the second-rate life and the oppressive forces of his own hometown. The Dalai Lama, it is important to note, had been on the national television news nine times during the month of March 1989 due to anti-Chinese rioting in Tibet. Followers of the Buddhist monk called for an independent Tibet, with the Dalai Lama renewing his appeals to Deng Xiaoping for action. As Rabbit tells his lover Thelma in April, "I've always kind of identified with him. He's about my age, I like to keep track of the guy. I have a gut feeling this'll be his year" (206). Rabbit's "gut feeling" is not, however (as historical research quickly reveals), a product of his fantasies or a guesswork exercise. The year 1989 was indeed the Dalai Lama's year, for he won the Nobel Peace Prize before it ended. Rabbit could not, however, have known that in April. Rabbit's "gut feeling" is thus a carefully arranged after-the-fact authorial intrusion, dictated by historical knowledge in order to make Rabbit's appropriation of the Dalai Lama's experience more complete and believable.

On May 16 Rabbit shows an even closer identification with the Dalai Lama. Through his usual metaphorical perception of the world, he first thinks of himself as one more brick in a number of buildings, or "one life in rows and walls and blocks of lives" (294), a part of the Brewer community. He discovers, however, that this view is "hard to sustain over against his original and continuing impression that Brewer and all the world are just frills on himself, like the lace around a plump satin valentine, himself the heart of the universe, like the Dalai Lama" (294). Being a part is not enough; he has to be the center around which the rest of life revolves and on which the rest of life depends. The Dalai Lama's godhood is appropriated by Rabbit and translated as selfhood—an essence he somehow cannot renounce.

The S and L scandal was in the news throughout the year, and for Rabbit it is just one more example of what poor, irresponsible administration can do. In his hospital bed he receives his long-time friend Ronnie Harrison and asks him how his business is going. Ronnie is now an insurance agent and answers, "The S and L mess hurt some companies but not ours. At least people have stopped borrowing against their policies at five per cent and investing at ten the way they were. That was killing our figures" (307). Rabbit's appropriation of the experience goes in two directions: on the one hand, he wrongly believes that his advanced age has freed him from insurance agents trying to sell him insurance and that, as a consequence, he won't be affected by it; on the other hand, he expresses his discomfort that the S and L banks and the rest of the world are just like his lot, in debt and on the verge of bankruptcy, with administrators refusing to take responsibility for their misdeeds. The S and L scandal and the lot's scandal are in many ways identical.

Gorbachev's visit to China in mid-May, during the Tiananmen Square student protests, writes itself into the novel because of Rabbit's remaining apprehension over the end of the Cold War and the role being played by Gorbachev, the charismatic Russian leader who remains likable "despite that funny mark on his head shaped like Japan" (295). Because of historical constraints, Rabbit is only allowed to sense the coming of the end of the Cold War; however, he misses the Cold War even before its end materializes. His longing has to do with an apparent loss of purpose for America should the Cold War end. It is also accompanied by the real possibility that the communists may regroup and gain strength:

"You can never trust communists not to gang up on you" (310). Updike's use of the second person in Rabbit's pondering reveals that Gorbachev and China function not only as the others but as a narratorial device that makes Rabbit synonymous with America.

The presence of Manuel Noriega in the news is explained by Rabbit's appropriation of the war on drugs discourse. For Rabbit, Noriega is not just the president of another country but quite simply "that evil Noriega" (310) who refuses to step down, even though the American president tells him to do so. Rabbit is still suffering from the transition syndrome which affects him every time America elects a new president. He still misses Reagan and shares the doubt of many middle Americans about Bush's capacity to properly replace the former president. Reagan's monarchichal posture is being followed by someone too human, too vulgarized to be worthy of his respect. Yet as a good citizen, Rabbit (who voted for Bush) soon sanctions him as his president, and from then on Bush's war on drugs becomes his war; Bush's debt crisis becomes his crisis; Bush's anxieties become his anxieties. If Bush says that Noriega is one of the evil infiltrators of drugs into the country, then it must be so, and Rabbit supports him.

The month of June brought abortion back to the forefront of the news, with pro-choice marchers protesting throughout the country. Simultaneously at the lot—a microcosm of America—Rabbit, Benny, and Elvira have a long discussion of the issue. Rabbit's position is pro-life, although he claims that his mind isn't really into it. Benny, a Catholic, takes a pro-life position as well, and Elvira is emphatically pro-choice. The discussion is a good example of how Rabbit, although reflecting the nation's indecision on this issue, identifies with President Bush, whose pro-life position is frequently reiterated by the media. As with America's foreign enemies (communism, terrorism, and foreigners) abortion is presently the major force of a powerful internal "enemy"—the feminist movement. Rabbit's feeling is that this movement is helping to destabilize his country and his home, which motivates his taking the side of the nation's highest authority.

The novel's most complete metaphorical appropriation occurs during the Fourth of July parade when Rabbit marches dressed as Uncle Sam—the event being America as the idealization of its national self. Rabbit's nationalism is brought to its highest point as he hears Kate Smith sing "God Bless America." At that moment he feels "he has been lifted up to survey all human history" and that America is "the happiest . . . country the world has ever seen" (371). As befits the model middle American, Rabbit plays Uncle Sam with pride and conviction.

Around July 20, we learn of the crash of a United DC-10 in Sioux City, Iowa. This piece of news becomes associated with Thelma's death because both happen in the same week. To Rabbit, however, the event is presented as a contrast to everything else he has seen on television, and it reminds him that he is getting old. The DC-10 crash is described as the "first piece of news that summer that wasn't the twentieth anniversary of something—of Woodstock, the Manson murders, Chappaquidick, the moon landing" (372). Although the circumstances of the accident are described in some detail, Rabbit shows little feeling for the suffering of the passengers and crew members killed in the crash. For him, the accident belongs in the category of television shows, with the difference that it does not depend on "resurrected footage" (372). The present, thus, is used here to induce in Rabbit the awareness that more and more he is part of the old show.

In August, Pete Rose and two more airplane crashes are the major topical events in the novel, although most of the August subchapters deal with Mr. Shimada's visit to the lot and with the microcosmic version of the foreign debt and foreign trade deficit problems faced by America, especially in its relation to Japan.

The Pete Rose affair has already been discussed at length in this work. The two airplane crashes, however, deserve some attention here. The accidents happened during the first two weeks of August, and besides helping to establish the precise day Nelson returned from the rehabilitation clinic (Monday, August 14), the inclusion of these apparently disconnected events serves the purpose of adding sharpness to Rabbit's middleness. The deaths in these two small airplane crashes were of six-term Congressman Mickey Leland (in the mountains of Ethiopia, where he had been flying to a refugee camp on a humanitarian mission) and of Republican Congressman Larkin Smith (killed not in Louisiana as Updike's text suggests, but near Hattiesburg, Mississippi). Leland was known as a former Black Panther—a representative of one of Rabbit's oldest fears. Larkin Smith, on the other hand, although a novice in Congress, was known for his staunch conservatism in defense of law and order. Rabbit, the small-town, middle-class, race-centered Protestant, shows a closer ideological identification with Smith, yet the narrator chooses to avoid inferences and judgments in his report, probably in an attempt to realize Updike's maxim that "it is in the middles that extremes clash, where ambiguity restlessly lies" (Howard 11). That Rabbit cannot look at any event without considering the race, color, nationality, sex, and political ideology of the people involved is an indication of the centers around which his life has revolved and which have been hardening since the 1950s. It is also evident that, besides adding chronological precision to the actions in the novel, Updike chooses to refer to these two crashes because they are another reminder to his hero of the fate that awaits him.

The direct reference to topical events during the month of August ends with Voyager 2 flying past Neptune and into the confines of the solar system on August 26. This scientific adventure is discussed at some length during Rabbit and Ronnie's game of golf, and as a consequence the feat is described as being as fantastic as "sinking a putt from New York to Los Angeles" (411). The appropriation of the event resurfaces when Rabbit's Nitrostat medication makes the world around him "delicate and distant, like Neptune's rings" (419). Similarly, at the end of a frustrating subsequent encounter with his old friend Ronnie, Rabbit's emptiness parallels the emptiness found in outer space, as he is sickened by "Voyager taking those last shots of Neptune and then sailing into the void forever. How can you believe how much void there is?" (413). Once again Rabbit abstracts from the historical event that which speaks to his soul.

It should by now have become clear that as the chronology of the novel and the chronology of historical events unfold, the appropriation acquires new dimensions and shifts its focus. Nelson, for example, is seen by Rabbit as time passes to be an amalgamation of public characters. In December 1988, he is like Rock Hudson; in mid-April, Ollie North; at the end of April, Adolph Hitler; in August, Secretary of the Treasury Nicholas Brady; and early in September, Jim Bakker. Depending on what is in the news, Rabbit regards Nelson as being like one or another. Nelson's runny nose is like Rock Hudson's (and a symptom of AIDS); Nelson and Lyle's possible shredding of self-incriminatory evidence is seen as what Oliver North would do; Nelson's economic recovery plan for the lot is similar to Nicholas Brady's plan for the administration of world debt; and Nelson's religious discourse and affected behavior, after his recovery from drug addiction, turn him into an unreliable Jim Bakker (portrayed as someone who, at the first opportunity, will be having sex with his secretaries and be involved in frauds of all kinds).

On Thursday, August 31, Rabbit leaves Brewer and drives in his Celica to his condo in Florida. The car radio is on, and throughout the trip Rabbit listens either to news or to easy oldies.

One after the other, the pieces of news and the songs are "written" into the experiences of his life. Among the many pieces of news he hears, most are related to AIDS (CIA complicity in the AIDS epidemic); drugs (Bush's war on drugs speech, a bomb exploding in Colombia, the provisional government in Panama); international terrorism (the missing tritium and the new TNA bomb detector installed at JFK airport in New York); the fear of an increasing presence of blacks in American life (David Dinkins is chosen to be Democratic candidate for mayor of New York City and another black Miss America is elected); more airplane accidents (a French DC-10 crash in the Sahara and a USAir jet crash in New York); Bartlett Giamatti's death; and PTL televangelist Jim Bakker's collapse in court. Most of these have already been discussed and help us to appreciate how circumstantial and contemporary Updike's metaphors are meant to be.

Politically, as we have seen, Rabbit's loss of power at the lot parallels America's apparent loss of power in the world. Bush's plight with foreign debt, drugs, AIDS, and abortion becomes his own plight, played out on a microlevel at home and at the Springer Motors Toyota dealership. Washington has mortgaged the country just as Nelson and his wife have placed two mortgages on their home; the Japanese are pushing America around just as they are determining the rules at his lot; drugs are in the home of every American just as they are in his; AIDS is so widespread that it has become everybody's problem; and abortion is an aspect of feminism which is destabilizing relations in every state in the nation and in his life. In the same way that Rabbit appropriates the events of each day, he also appropriates the major issues of the decade.

If facts are indeed like letters that we use to make words, as Updike wants us to believe, it is clear that the metaphoric trope is what determines the rules for putting these letters together and constructing words which assure us that Rabbit's world is never one of total strangeness. In fact, the whole novel may be said to be a metaphoric apprehension of America in the 1980s through a mind whose values find their bedrock in the 1950s; a mind which, through gradual and constant appropriation of the off-center historical forces in subsequent decades, has brought the new, the foreign, the different, the subversive, and the dangerous to the safe and narrow limits of middleness.

A few comments still remain to be made on the synechdochic trope—how it operates in the novel and how it makes Rabbit tick. Whereas metaphor strives toward bringing the new and antagonistic into familiarity, synechdoche, being the trope of ideology, offers itself as a field to be sowed by the world of facts. Synechdoche thus defines itself as the stage upon which the historical actors and agents of the present have their actions performed and evaluated.

In light of the foregoing discussion, I believe we can affirm that from an ideological perspective Rabbit has not changed very much during the course of the tetralogy and that in general terms he is the same character we first met in 1959. He is still fundamentally the man in the middle, placed there by the ideological forces which shaped him throughout the age of consensus—the 1950s. Nationalism, anticommunism, racism, sexism, authoritarianism, and individualism are still the predominant forces underlying his thoughts and actions. What has changed are the facts and external circumstances which he has to deal with on a daily basis. But these daily challenges, though seemingly a menace in the present, pose no real threat of ideological mutation. In the long run, they will (as always) be absorbed and processed by the ideology of middleness in its endless effort to redefine and reenergize itself.

This premise is not the generally acknowledged reading of Updike's text and challenges, for example, Sanford Pinsker's review of *Rabbit at Rest*. Pinsker argues that "what changes in the last novel is Rabbit himself, although in nuanced ways more subtle than those readings hoping for a 'better' Rabbit might prefer. Clearly he remains self-centered and selfish, vaguely racist and sexist, materialistic and politically conventional [but] more reflective, more genuinely philosophical than he was [in the earlier novels]" (735).

As we have seen again and again in the preceding chapters, Rabbit remains not vaguely but aggressively and adamantly racist and sexist, and his reflections are, for the most part, simply reactions to the presentness of circumstances and actions around him. His philosophy, as a consequence, is only as genuine as the scene, past and present, in which and through which he lives—no more and no less. Pinsker does admit that Rabbit is the typical middle American, but his reading does not account for how instinctive and impulsive a character Rabbit in fact is and how little he depends on his own ideas to exist. What brings Rabbit to life are the forces of the American scene. These forces, through the antagonisms they evoke, challenge the ideology of middleness and make us perceive that middleness, no matter how much it is taken for granted, is always there and firmly entrenched.

Not all of the historical forces are present with equal intensity in the novel. Preference is largely determined by the ideological substratum which pre-defines Rabbit even before he is exposed to his local or national milieu. The present, therefore, does not define his ideology but illuminates it, reinforces it, and challenges it. Born into the present with a clearly defined past, Rabbit is ultimately crystalized ideology in interaction with the multiple voices of historical reality. To speak of Rabbit's ideological characteristics, therefore, is to abstract facets of historical reality highlighted during the process of his immersion in the American scene.

Authoritarianism is one of these facets. It is a core concept which expresses itself through nationalism, bellicosity, anti-communism, racism, and sexism. It insinuates itself in relationships where domination and preservation of power are the major goals. The solid citizen of the sixties and the Rotary Club member of the seventies still feels guilty for suggesting to little Judy that the police are too lazy to enforce traffic regulations. He quickly changes "lazy" to "busy" as the empathetic narrator tells us that Rabbit has always been "one to defend the authorities" (263). In Rabbit's mind, criticism of authorities and, *a fortiori*, of everything these authorities represent is tantamount to heresy. His blind admiration for Ronald Reagan; his objection to the depiction of George Bush as too normal a human being; his support for causes which will maintain the status quo, both nationally and internationally; his fear of feminists, communists, blacks, and foreigners—all are expressions of his need to assert and preserve authority, not as a result of logical problematizations but as an expression of loyalty to his synthesis of the Establishment's guidelines, openly or subliminally handed to him and appropriated by him throughout the decades.

Individualism, on the other hand, can be read in two ways in the novel, first, as a disproportionate emphasis on private interest and as an impulsive antagonism toward everything which threatens to confuse the individual with the collective. It is thus not an affirmation of individuality but an individuality so much in love with itself that it cannot tolerate differences or truly concern itself with the needs and sensitivities of others. With feminists-to-be like his wife Janice and Elvira around him (and with women in general viewed as a social category), this brand of individualism translates into sexism.

Rabbit's relationship with Thelma better defines this ideological trait at the interpersonal level:

> Their relationship at the very start was established with her in pursuit of him, and all the years since, of hidden meetings, of wise decisions to end it and thrilling abject collapses back into sex, *have not disrupted the fundamental pattern of her giving and his taking*, of her fearing their end more than he, and clinging, and disliking herself for clinging, and wanting to punish him for her dislike, and him shrugging and continuing to bask in the sun of her love, that rises every day whether he is there or not. He can't believe it, quite, and has to keep testing her. (200, my emphasis)

Contrary to what one may think, with Rabbit this pattern of behavior does not exhaust itself in interpersonal relations. Since the Dalai Lama is again conveniently in the papers,[1] this historical figure is put to the service of Rabbit's idea that he is still, as Thelma complains, "the center of the universe" (206). As he broods about his life, Rabbit (certainly stimulated by the always present forces of history) "wonders [whether] you still believe in God, if people keep telling you you are God?" (103). In his question we can hear clear echoes of Rabbit's waning religiosity and especially of Reverend Eccles, who in 1959 suggested that Rabbit gave faith to people. Rabbit's self-centered behavior, a popular perversion of the traditional American emphasis on individuality, has more to do with the Cold War spirit than with Emerson or Thoreau. The Dalai Lama is present in the Rabbit novels not because of his brand of religion or because of his influence on American thought but because he became a symbol of resistance against the forces of communism. Since this is a war not yet over,

---

[1] The Dalai Lama, who in 1959 during Rabbit's drive south was escaping the communist Chinese forces, was again in the news during the month of April 1989 because of the pro-independence riots in Tibet. On April 1, 1989, the *New York Times* reports that more than three hundred Tibetans were in detention since martial law had been imposed at the beginning of March of that year.

the readers are invited to pay attention to and read into the story the actions of the communists in China in the 1980s.

The second way of looking at individualism has to do with the appropriation by Rabbit of the specific interests emphasized by the country. Every time Rabbit and America become synonymous, his individualism expresses itself as nationalism, otherness becoming in the process not other individuals but other nations. Again, it is not an affirmation of national identity that occurs but an extrapolation of this identity to limits within which he can only define himself in aggressive opposition to the rest of the world. The pattern of his relationship with Thelma, for example, is almost identical to what Mr. Shimada sees as America's problem; that is, the country is behaving selfishly, crying and complaining without producing, indulging in debt, living in such a way that "nothing comes out, all goes in—foreign goods, foreign capital. America take everything, give nothing. Rike big brack hole" (390). In other words, to the extent that Rabbit becomes America, his individualism transmutes itself into nationalism.

The same could be said of his perception of himself as a member of the white race and of the male sex. When his individualism manifests itself through identifications which surpass the realm of the interpersonal, Rabbit starts perceiving the other sex and the other races as threatening, not only to himself but to a national way of life. Thus, showing Elvira (the female) her place can be read as a smaller dimension of his concern with the national dispute over abortion and the presence of women in the labor market; his daily promenades into the black neighborhood of Deleon and his remarkable concern with New York City's mayoral election are, similarly, materializations of his protest against his exclusion from America's inner cities. Both sexism and racism can then also be understood as different realms of expression for a frame of mind which has hardened certain cores of reference and which produces instances of identity capable of marginalizing whatever is not male, white, American, and capitalist.

The religiosity which was clearly present in the fifties has a much less significant status in the eighties. Rabbit, who already had doubts about Reverend Eccles's secularized version of God, forgot religion completely in the sixties. Instead the black Vietnam War veteran Skeeter became his preacher. Updike, who in earlier manuscript versions had brought Eccles back as a homosexual, excluded him completely from *Rabbit Redux*. In the seventies, Rabbit's God had shrunk to the size of a raisin. To make matters worse, the raisin got lost under the car seat. In other words, Rabbit's God was still around but hardly noticeable, and the minister of the church (another version of Eccles) had become a homosexual.

Things are not very different in the eighties. Rabbit still does not go to church often and thinks God "is like a friend you've had so long you've forgotten what you liked about him" (450). Unlike Thelma and Ronnie, who have become religious these last years "to help the panic" (205), Rabbit, who "used to be religious in a funny way" (309), shows his cynicism is growing with age. The PTL scandal which led to the trial of televangelist Jim Bakker on twenty-four counts of fraud and sexual harassment occupies almost a whole page of the novel. The trial continued throughout 1989, revealing, as the CBS *Evening News* put it, "a kingdom of excess" with some of its members living "like royalty," spending as much as $2000 a month to pay the electric bills to keep the swimming pool permanently heated at ninety degrees. Jim Bakker made the front page of the *New York Times* on September 1, 1989, at the time Rabbit was driving south trying to escape judgment and punishment for having had sex, not with his secretary, but with his son's wife.

Rabbit does seem to remain religious in a curious yet ideologically consistent way. As suits a man in the middle, he hates marginal sects like the one to which Thelma and Ronnie now belong. Although Rabbit enjoys seeing the license plates reading "You've Got a Friend in Jesus" (182), on which the name Jesus replaces "Pennsylvania," he cannot stick to the radio station where the minister repeatedly insists, as if talking to him, that "Jesus knows! Jesus looks into your heart! Jesus sees the death in your heart!" (459). He prefers instead a love song from his Army days. He dismisses this preacher as he dismisses the southern "fanatics" (449) who are protesting a recent court ban on organized prayer at football games.[2] As he sees it, these protests are marginal and do not deserve his respect.

It is finally curious to notice that Reverend Jerry Falwell's Moral Majority, whose purpose since 1979 had been to mobilize the religious right on such issues as abortion, divorce, teenage pregnancy, school prayer, drug abuse, and pornography, was officially dissolved on June 11, 1989. Reverend Falwell declared his mission accomplished despite the fact that the problems continued. He argued, however, that "the religious right is solidly in place and, like the galvanizing of the black church as a political force a generation ago, the religious conservatives in America are now in for the duration."[3] Since Rabbit, like Reagan and Bush, would have strongly identified with Falwell's agenda, it does seem curious that this news was not incorporated into the story. The chronology of *Rabbit at Rest* gives us one technical explanation. Chapter II ends on May 10 and Chapter III starts on June 19, so the period from May 11 to June 18 is not covered by the novel. Whatever the explanation may be, the fact remains that the Moral

---

[2] This piece of news about the uproar and defiance in hundreds of southern towns against the decision to ban prayer at football games was reported by the *New York Times* edition of September 2, 1989.

Majority is present in *Rabbit at Rest* in absentia through the issues raised and the stands taken on those issues. It is like the noisy silence that creeps into Rabbit's loneliness, or "the presence of absence" (493), to follow the narrator's deconstructive gist.

These are, then, the major ideological forces at work in the novel. They besiege the axes of story and history, of narrator and reader, and through their affirmations and denials create a focus, a point and a horizon of attention, around which and through which the contingent forces of life and death circulate. The frontiers of history and story, fact and fiction, background and foreground become more and more tenuous as we realize that Rabbit is as much one as the other.

In conclusion, the scene-centered reading of *Rabbit at Rest* in particular and of the Rabbit tetralogy as a whole is essential to perceive how Rabbit comes to life and how much his story is the story of middle America. The Rabbit of the 1980s, as we have seen, has remained fundamentally identical to the Rabbit of the 1950s—an identity which serves the purpose of unveiling the essential ideological characteristics of middle America. What has changed is not Rabbit but the scene in which he operates and in which he is exposed to different social, political, cultural, and economic realities, along with new styles, fads, and emphases. Yet as with the previous novels, the scene of *Rabbit at Rest* has been carefully texturized to match the ideological needs of the depicted protagonist—needs which had been defined even before the story was written and which are illuminated at every step of Rabbit's trajectory through history.

Updike's text, with all its memorabilia, time and space referents, and use of historically-placed metaphors, is an invitation to historicize on every page. The reader, especially the contemporary and well-informed reader, will invariably contribute to the

---

[3] In the *New York Times*, June 12, 1989.

"writing" of the text and will participate in the identification of the permanent underlying conflict between the forces of middleness and their natural antagonists. These conflicts, at every decade's end, are temporarily pushed to a crisis, forcing a renegotiation of the terms upon which Rabbit's social relations will be set. Each of the Rabbit novels is a synoptic portrayal of these historicized crises in which middleness tries to neutralize the more radical antagonisms and make adjustments to bring into the system whatever it considers acceptable.

Rabbit's all-pervading fear of death in the eighties is, thus, also the fear that the days of his and America's empire are gradually coming to an end. Rabbit is alarmed to find out that one of the predictions in the history book he is reading, namely that "America . . . was formed for happiness, but not for empire" (86), may eventually come true. He realizes that America, like himself, is no longer "the big cheese." This loss of power (although at times a relief) is ultimately frightening. It is a form of death—something which, despite Rabbit's frequent flirtation with suicide and the many intimations of mortality around him, is rejected by his last effort to win. Rabbit is not dead yet, and the middle American educated in the fifties, though somewhat uneasy in these post–Cold War days, is still alive and strong. At the end of the 1990s, we may not be surprised to find that Rabbit is in Pennsylvania, Miami, or Boston, alive and at home—his home—America.

# BIBLIOGRAPHY

Berryman, Charles. *Decade of Novels—Fiction of the 1970s: Forms and Challenge*. Troy, New York: Whitston, 1990.

Blake, Davis H., and Robert S. Walters. *The Politics of Global Economic Relations*. Englewood Cliffs: Prentice-Hall, 1987.

Burchard, Rachael D. *John Updike: Yea Sayings*. Carbondale: Southern Illinois University Press, 1971.

Burgess, Anthony. "Language, Myth, and Mr. Updike." *Commonweal* 83 (1966): 557–59.

Burke, Kenneth. *A Grammar of Motives*. Berkeley: University of California Press, 1945.

Burns, Timothy, ed. *After History?* Lanham, Maryland: Rowman & Littlefield, 1994.

Burhans Jr., Clinton. "Things Falling Apart: Structure and Theme in *Rabbit, Run*." *Studies in the Novel* 5 (1973): 336–51.

Bush, George. "Drug-War Speech." In *Historic Documents of 1989*, edited by Hoyt Gimlin. Washington: Congressional Quarterly, 1990.

Campbell, Jeff. "Middling, Hidden, Troubled America: John Updike's Rabbit Tetralogy." *Journal of the American Studies Association of Texas* 24 (October 1993): 26–45.

Carper, Gordon N., and Joyce Carper. *The Meaning of History*. Westport, Connecticut: Greenwood Press, 1991.

Carr, Edward Hallet. *What is History?* New York: Vintage, 1961.

Chafe, William H., and Harvard Sitkoff, eds. *A History of Our Time: Readings on Postwar America*. New York: Oxford University Press, 1983.

Clausen, Jan. "Native Fathers." *Kenyon Review* 14, no. 2 (1992): 45–55.

Chomsky, Noam. *Toward a New Cold War*. New York: Pantheon Books, 1982.

Crews, Frederick. *The Critics Bear It Away: American Fiction and the Academy*. New York: Random, 1992.

DeBellis, Jack. "The Awful Power: John Updike's Use of Kubrick's *2001: A Space Odyssey* in *Rabbit Redux*." *Literature/Film Quarterly* 21, no. 3 (1993): 209–17.

Detweiler, Robert. *John Updike*. New York: Twayne, 1972.

Edwards, Thomas R. "Updike's Rabbit Trilogy." Review of *Rabbit Is Rich,* by John Updike. *Atlantic* 248 (1981): 94–102.

Ellison, James. "Rabbit is Buying Krugerrands." Review of *Rabbit Is Rich,* by John Updike. *Psychology Today* 15 (1981): 110–115.

Enright, D. J. "The Inadequate American: John Updike's Fiction." In *Conspirators and Poets*. London: Chatto & Windus, 1966.

Fukuyama, Francis. "The End of History." *The National Interest* 16 (Summer 1989): 3–18.

Garner, Dwight. "The Salon Interview." *Salon* 8 (1996): 2.

Garruth, Gorton. *The Encyclopedia of American Facts and Dates*. New York: Harper-Collins, 1993.

Giles, James R. *American Novelists Since World War II*. Detroit: Gales Research, 1994.

Gimlin, Hoyt, ed. *Historic Documents of 1989*. Washington: Congressional Quarterly, 1990.

Goyal, Vinod. "Beyond Contending Approaches: A New International Economic Regime." *Hindu*, January 20–21, 1995, section C, p. 1.

Gray, Paul. "A Crisis in Confidence." Review of *Rabbit Is Rich,* by John Updike. *Time* 118 (October 1981): 90.

Greiner, Donald J. *The Other John Updike*. Athens: Ohio University Press, 1981.

_____. *John Updike's Novels*. Athens: Ohio University Press, 1984.

_____. "John Updike." In *American Novelists Since World War II*, edited by James R. Giles, 250–276. Detroit: Gale Research Inc., 1994.

Hamilton, Alice and Kenneth Hamilton. *The Elements of John Updike*. Grand Rapids: William B. Erdmans, 1970.

Hanson, Jim. *The Next Cold War?—American Alternatives for the Twenty-First Century*. West Port, Connecticut: Praeger, 1996.

Henderson, Lesley, ed. *Contemporary Novelists*. Chicago: St. James Press, 1991.

Hicks, Thomas. "Updike's Rabbit Novels: An American Epic." *Sacred Heart University Review* 13, no. 1–2 (1993): 65–70.

Howard, Jane. "Can a Nice Novelist Finish First?" In *Conversations with John Updike*, edited by James Plath. Jackson: University Press of Mississippi, 1994.

Kennedy, Eileen. "*Rabbit Redux*." Review of *Rabbit Redux*, by John Updike. *Best Sellers* 31 (December 1971): 429.

Klinkowitz, Jerome. "John Updike's America." *North American Review* 265 (September 1980): 68–71.

_____. *Literary Subversions: New American Fiction and the Practice of Criticism*. Carbondale: Southern Illinois University Press, 1985.

Lathrop, Kathleen. "Updike on America: The Expanding Vision of John Updike in his Post-Olinger Novels." Ph.D. diss., New York State University, 1984.

Lesniack, James G. *Contemporary Authors*. Detroit: Gale Research, 1991.

Levy, Peter B. *Encyclopedia of the Reagan-Bush Years*. Westport, Connecticut: Greenwood Press, 1996.

Lewis, Anthony. "The Cost of Reagan." *New York Times*, September 7, 1989, sec. A, p. 27.

Mallon, Thomas. "Rabbit, Jog." *National Review* 33 (1981): 356–58.

Markham, James. "Unpredictable Russians Boggle West's Brain." *New York Times*, December 27, 1988, sec. A, p.2.

Markle, Joyce B. *Fighters and Lovers: Theme in the Novels of John Updike*. New York: New York University Press, 1973.

Martin, Jay. "Caught in Fantasyland: Electronic Media's Hold on Society." *USA Today Magazine* 117 (July 1988): 92–93.

*Modern Fiction Studies* 35 (Winter 1989): 771-72.

Morales, Waltraud Queiser. "The War on Drugs: A New U. S. National Security Doctrine?" *Third World Quarterly* 3 (1989): 147–169.

Newman, Judie. *"Rabbit at Rest:* The Return of the Work Ethic." In *Rabbit Tales:Poetry and Politics in John Updike's Rabbit Quartet,* edited by Lawrence Broer. Tuscaloosa: Alabama State University Press, forthcoming.

O'Connell, Mary. *Updike and the Patriarchal Dilemma: Masculinity in the Rabbit Novels.* Carbondale: Southern Illinois University Press, 1996.

O'Connell, Shaun. "Rabbits Remembered." *Massachusetts Review* 15 (1974): 511–520.

Olster, Stacey. "Rabbit Rerun: Updike's Replay of Popular Culture in *Rabbit at Rest.*" *Modern Fiction Studies* 37, no. 1 (1991): 45–59.

Pinsker, Sanford. "Review of *Rabbit at Rest,* by John Updike." *Georgia Review* 4 (1990): 734–35.

_____. "Joyce's Poldy/Updike's Rabbit: Popular Culture and the Problem of Consciousness." *Cimarron Review* 110 (January 1995): 92-101.

_____. "An Interview with John Updike." *Sewanee Review* 104, no. 3 (1996): 423–433.

Plath, James. *Conversations with John Updike.* Jackson: University Press of Mississippi, 1994.

Pritchett, V. S. "Updike." Review of *Rabbit Is Rich*, by John Updike. *New Yorker*, November 9, 1981: 201–202.

Raymont, Henry. "John Updike Completes a Sequel to *Rabbit, Run*." *New York Times*, July 27, 1971.

Reagan, Ronald. "Farewell Address." In *Historic Documents of 1989*, edited by Hoyt Gimlin. Washington: Congressional Quarterly, 1990.

Regan, R. A. "Updike's Symbol of the Center." *Modern Fiction Studies* 20, no. 1 (1974): 77–96.

Ristoff, Dilvo I. *Updike's America: The Presence of Contemporary American History in John Updike's Rabbit Trilogy*. New York: Peter Lang, 1988.

Samuels, Charles. "Updike on the Present." Review of *Rabbit Redux*, by John Updike. *New Republic* 165 (1971): 29–30.

Seethuraman, Ramchandran. "Writing Woman's Body: Male Fantasy, Desire and Sexual Identity in Updike's *Rabbit, Run*." *Literature Interpretation Theory* 2 (1993): 101–22.

Simes, Dimitri K. "If the Cold War Is Over, Then What?" *New York Times*, December 27, 1988, sec A, p. 12.

Sloan, Dave. *Baseball Guide*. St. Louis: The Sporting News, 1990.

Sloer de Godfrid, Fanny, et al. "Los Estados Unidos y los Personajes Femininos en las Novelas de 'Rabbit.' " *Proceedings* of 26 *Jornadas en la Facultad de Filosofía y Letras,* Universidad de Buenos Aires: November 1993.

Sorkin, Adam, ed. *Politics and the Muse: Studies in the Politics of Recent American Literature.* Bowling Green: Popular, 1989.

Stern, Fritz, ed. *The Varieties of History.* New York: Meridian Books, 1956.

Stubbs, John C. "The Search for Perfection in *Rabbit, Run.*" *Critique: Studies in Modern Fiction* 10 (1968): 94–101.

Sulzberger, Arthur O. *The New York Times Page One.* New York: The New York Times Company, 1993.

Tarnoff, Peter. "A Bizarre Nostalgia for the Cold War." *New York Times,* September 19, 1988, sec. A, p. 12.

Taylor, Larry E. *Pastoral and Anti-Pastoral in John Updike's Fiction.* Carbondale: Southern Illinois University Press, 1971.

Thornburn, David, and Howard Eiland. *John Updike: A Collection of Critical Essays.* Englewood Cliffs: Prentice-Hall, 1979.

Trachtenberg, Stanley, ed. *New Essays on Rabbit, Run.* Cambridge: Cambridge University Press, 1993.

Trueheart, Charles. "Sex, God and John Updike." *Washington Post,* October 28, 1990, sec F, p. 1.

Updike, John. *Rabbit at Rest.* New York: Knopf, 1990.

_____. "Why Rabbit Had to Go." *New York Times Book Review*, August 5, 1990, sec. 7, p. 1

_____. "On Not Being a Dove." *Commentary* 87, no. 3 (1989): 22–30.

_____. "The Plight of the American Writer." *Change* 12 (October 1977): 36–41.

_____. *Self-Consciousness.* New York: Knopf, 1989.

_____. *Memories of the Ford Administration.* New York: Knopf, 1992.

_____. *Rabbit Angstrom.* New York: Knopf, 1995.

Uphaus, Suzanne Henning. *John Updike.* New York: Frederick Ungar, 1980.

Vargo, Edward P. "Cornchips, Catheters, Toyotas: The Making of History in *Rabbit at Rest.*" In *Rabbit Tales: Poetry and Politics in John Updike's Rabbit Quartet,* edited by Lawrence Broer. Mobile: Alabama State University Press, forthcoming.

Vaugh, Philip H. *John Updike's Images of America.* Reseda, California: Mojave Books, 1982.

Veeser, H. Aram, ed. *The New Historicism.* New York: Routledge, 1989.

Wade, Kevin. *Working Girl.* Filmscript. Hollywood: Script City, 1987.

Warren, Donald. *The Radical Center: Middle Americans and the Politics of Alienation.* Notre Dame: University of Notre Dame Press, 1976.

White, Hayden. *The Uses of History.* Detroit: Wayne University Press, 1968.

_____. *Metahistory: The Historical Imagination in Nineteenth-Century Europe.* Baltimore: Johns Hopkins University Press, 1973.

_____. *Tropics of Discourse: Essays in Cultural Criticism.* Baltimore: Johns Hopkins University Press, 1978.

_____. *The Content of the Form: Narrative Discourse and Historical Representation.* Baltimore: Johns Hopkins University Press, 1987.

Williams, Don. "Updike Run." In *Writer's Yearbook* 66, edited by Thomas Clark. Cincinnati: F & W Publications, 1995.

Wilson, Mathew. "The Rabbit Tetralogy: From Solitude to Society to Solitude Again." *Modern Fiction Studies* 37, no. 1 (1991): 5–24.

World Bank. *World Development Report 1988.* New York: Oxford University Press, 1988.

_____. *World Development Report 1989.* New York: Oxford University Press, 1989.

# APPENDIX 1

## *RABBIT AT REST:*
## A CHRONOLOGY OF STORY AND HISTORY

| DATE | HISTORICAL REFERENCES |
|------|----------------------|

### DECEMBER 27, 1988—TUESDAY[1]

1. Rabbit and Janice pick up their son Nelson, their daughter-in-law Pru, and their two grandchildren Judy (eight years old) and Roy (four years old), at the Miami airport;

2. Rabbit and Judy go to buy candy at an airport store and can't find where their

1. Death of television anchorman Max Robinson, of AIDS;

2. Death of singer Roy Orbison;

3. Explosion of PanAm flight 103 over Scotland;

4. Accident with jet flying from Rochester to Atlanta;

---

[1] In the Introduction to *Rabbit Angstrom* Updike claims the novel starts on December 28. Since the novel starts on a Tuesday, however, December 27 is the correct date.

Camry Deluxe wagon is parked;

3. Grandchildren want to go to Disneyland and are unhappy when Rabbit tells them it is too far;

4. Arrival at Valhalla Village, the Angstrom's condo in Deleon, Florida, bought in 1984; quarrel about sleeping arrangements;

5. Rabbit and Nelson discuss the lot, the car business, and the Japanese;

6. Pru, Janice, and the kids go to the swimming pool;

7. Rabbit and Janice return from the pool early; quarrel over stat sheets which disappeared and which Janice half admits she threw out.

5. Reference to Theodore Bundy on death row in Florida;

6. Reference to dying Japanese Emperor Hirohito;

7. Reference to pregnant woman killed in Florida;

8. Reference to Japanese buying American property all over the United States.

## DECEMBER 28, 1988—WEDNESDAY

1. First fight of the day: Judy wants to go to Disneyworld;

2. Rabbit presents his plan for today and tomorrow;

3. Rabbit notices Nelson's

1. Reference to film *Working Girl*;

2. Reference to television show *Today*;

3. Reference to Donald Trump;

nose is always running and thinks of Rock Hudson and AIDS;

4. Rabbit plays golf with his Jewish friends; Janice, Pru and the kids go shopping, have lunch at Burger King, swim, and play shuffleboard and cards;

5. Rabbit and his friends discuss Deion Sanders, Bush, Dukakis, Reagan, and the PanAm accident;

6. Nelson drives around town looking for drugs;

7. Rabbit takes an afternoon nap as Janice goes to a women's group meeting;

8. Rabbit watches bits of many television programs as Judy switches from channel to channel;

9. They go to dinner without Nelson, who is still driving around Florida looking for drugs;

10. Judy reveals during dinner that her father "a lot of times doesn't have any money. Bills come and even men keep coming to the house and Mommy can't pay them"

4. Deion Sanders arrested in Florida for assault and battery on a policeman;

5. Reference to greenhouse effect;

6. Reference to Bush's "no more taxes" proposal and his attacks on Michael Dukakis during the last presidential campaign;

7. Reference to Reagan's legacy;

8. Reference to Bush hunting quail in Texas;

9. More on PanAm accident;

10. Reference to *The Jeffersons*, *The Wonder Years*, *Night Court*, and other television programs.

(82);

11. Rabbit, with Judy switching channels all the time, watches *The Return of Martin Guerre,* starring Gerard Depardieu;

12. Rabbit reads himself to sleep;

13. Nelson returns at 1:00 A.M.

## DECEMBER 29, 1988—THURSDAY

1. Inspired by the Depardieu movie, Rabbit thinks of Janice as a total stranger (first conflict of the day);

2. At 9:30 A.M. Rabbit, Janice, Judy, and Roy start on a visit to Thomas Alva Edison's winter home and the Sarasota Jungle Gardens;

3. Rabbit gives Judy a sadistic squeeze;

4. They have lunch at a McDonald's with a closed playground, so Roy throws a fit;

5. Judy teases Roy for crying during *Dumbo*;

6. Rabbit sees bo-tree like a Buddha and thinks of the Da-

1. Reference to Ethiopian famine;

2. More on PanAm flight 103;

3. More on Deion Sanders;

4. Reference to pollution in Lake Okeechobee;

5. Reference to the film *Dumbo,* with brief summary;

6. Reference to the Dalai Lama;

7. Reference to the movie *Working Girl,* with brief summary;

8. Reference to documentary about foreigners buying up American businesses.

lai Lama;

7. Rabbit accidentally eats bird food;

8. Rabbit, Janice, Judy, and Roy watch *Working Girl;* Roy and Rabbit do not see movie to the end;

9. Janice announces that she wants to be a working girl;

10. Pru cooks grilled snook for dinner and explains about cholesterol;

11. Rabbit looks forward to the departure of his guests.

## DECEMBER 30, 1988—FRIDAY

1. Based on what Pru tells him, Rabbit thinks Nelson may have AIDS;

2. Rabbit and Judy go sailing; the boat capsizes and Judy can't be seen;

3. Rabbit saves Judy and has a heart attack;

4. At 12:25 P.M. Janice is informed that Rabbit was taken to the hospital.

1. Reference to popular children's songs, many of them sung in part by Judy;

2. Reference to last September's Americas Cup;

3. Reference to Arab terrorists who are compared to contemporary baseball players;

4. Reference to Deion Sanders;

5. Reference to Lake Okechobee's pollution;

6. Reference to corruption involving the head of Cape

Coral's police narcotics team;

7. Reference to Florida as hottest place in the country;

8. Reference to television series *Miami Vice*.

## DECEMBER 31, 1988—SATURDAY

1. Rabbit at Deleon Community General Hospital; perceives the "world around him as gaseous and rising" and himself "at the still center of a new world";

2. Janice, Pru, Nelson, Judy, and Roy visit Rabbit at the hospital;

3. Pru tells Nelson she won't sleep with him because she is afraid of getting AIDS;

4. Nelson, Pru, and their children leave for Brewer, Pennsylvania.

1. Reagan and Bush get subpoenas;

2. Reference to diminishing crime rates in the region;

3. More on PanAm flight 103;

4. Reference to fog during football game between the Eagles and the Bears at Soldier's Field in Chicago;

5. Reference to *The Cosby Show* and various other television shows; reference to various television commercials;

6. Reference to films *Breakfast at Tiffany's, Casablanca, Little Big Horn, The Fists of Bruce Lee*;

7. More about PanAm flight 103;

8. Reference to Barry Manilow;

9. More on Deion Sanders.

## APRIL 10, 1989—MONDAY

1. Rabbit drives around Brewer, observing the spring and changes in the town, "freshening his memory and hurting himself with the pieces of his old self that cling to almost every corner of the Brewer area";

2. Janice begins looking for a job;

3. Rabbit thinks of his past and remembers his dead father and mother-in-law.

1. Reference to the new Pennsylvania license plates and telephone directory;

2. Reference to guys in prison who bite guards to give them AIDS;

3. Reference to the movie *Working Girl*;

4. Reference to planet Saturn;

5. Reference to Princess Di;

6. Reference to the John Hinckley trial.

## APRIL 18, 1989—TUESDAY

1. Rabbit visits his lover Thelma Harrison;

2. We learn that Thelma is very ill, that her illness has cost the Harrisons a fortune, and that they are no longer members of their old club, The Flying Eagle;

3. Thelma reveals that she knows Nelson is a cocaine addict;

1. Reference to yuppies;

2. Reference to the Dalai Lama;

3. Reference to Paraguay's dictator, Stroessner;

4. Reference to HIV and to the discovery that it may remain dormant for up to ten years;

5. Reference to AIDS drugs; criticism of FDA's restrictions

4. Rabbit refuses to have sex with Thelma and confesses that he is afraid of catching AIDS;

5. Thelma informs Rabbit that she and her husband have become members of a new marginal religious sect;

6. Half an hour after leaving Thelma's home, Rabbit visits the lot, where he discovers that Nelson has taken down "the old blown-up photos of Harry in his glory days as a basketball star, with the headlines calling him 'Rabbit'"; Rabbit also discovers that Nelson has hired a woman, Elvira Ollenbach, and an Italian-American, Benny Leone, as salespersons;

7. Rabbit meets Lyle, the lot's accountant, who is a homosexual and has AIDS; Lyle refuses to show him the books, arguing that he can only show them to authorized persons (that is, to Nelson, his boss, or to Janice, the owner of the company);

8. Rabbit drives home and hears on the radio news about over imports of new drugs; criticism of the Reagan administration's homophobia;

6. Reference to baseball player Mike Schmidt;

7. Reference to television show *Jeopardy*;

8. Phillies playing the Mets;

9. Reference to Oliver North's shredding of self-incriminatory evidence during the Iran-Contra scandal;

10. Reference to Dale Berra's arrest on charges of buying drugs from a cocaine ring.

his old baseball hero Mike
Schmidt;

9. At home in the evening
Rabbit and Janice talk about
their son's drug addiction;

10. Janice is excited about the
real estate courses she is taking at the Penn State extension;

11. Rabbit informs her that
he visited the lot in the afternoon, that Nelson wasn't
there, and that he has hired
"one fag, one wop, and a
skirt";

12. Rabbit informs Janice that
Lyle would not let him see the
lot's accounts without her
authorization;

13. Rabbit tells Janice that he
thinks Nelson takes cocaine,
bleeds the company, and that
Nelson and Lyle may shred
the evidence of wrongdoing;

14. Rabbit and Janice consider their own guilt in Nelson's drug addiction;

15. Rabbit and Janice receive
threatening phone calls from
drug dealers because of Nelson's debts.

## APRIL 19, 1989—WEDNESDAY

1. Phone calls from drug dealers to Rabbit and Janice inform them that their "son has incurred serious debts," and they threaten to do physical harm to Nelson and his family.

1. No direct reference to topical events is made, although America's drug problem is at stake.

## APRIL 20, 1989—THURSDAY

1. Rabbit seeks advice from his friend Charlie Stavros;

2. Rabbit and Charlie discuss the meaning of all these accidents;

3. Rabbit and Charlie discuss the change of mores in Brewer and the possible influence of drugs on the younger generation;

4. Rabbit asks Charlie to talk to Janice about Nelson's drug addiction and about Lyle's refusal to show the lot's books.

1. Reference to Mike Schmidt's performance in game played against the Pirates in Three Rivers Stadium;

2. More on PanAm flight 103;

3. Reference to soccer fans crushed in Sheffield, England.

4. Reference to the explosion aboard battleship *Iowa*;

5. Truck driver from West Miami caught near Maiden Springs with amount of cocaine worth millions.

## APRIL 29, 1989—SATURDAY

1. After being physically attacked by Nelson, who was under the influence of cocaine, Pru calls Rabbit and Janice for help at 2:10 A.M.;

2. Rabbit and Janice drive over to Nelson's home; on the way, Janice tries to convince Rabbit that Pru might be over-dramatizing things because she has her own agenda (getting rid of Nelson);

3. Nelson accuses Rabbit of playing sexist games at the lot; Rabbit tells Nelson he is a mess and a menace and accuses Nelson of letting the Mafia into the lot by hiring an Italian;

4. Rabbit compares Nelson to Hitler;

5. Janice and Nelson talk about his drug problem and the financial crisis at the lot;

6. Rabbit and Janice drive home at around 4:00 A.M., arguing all the way home; Rabbit is in a punitive mood; Janice tries to be more understanding of her son.

1. Reference to former Nazi leader Adolph Hitler;

2. Reference to South American debt;

3. Reference to S and L banks scandal.

standing of her son.

## MAY 12, 1989—FRIDAY

1. Rabbit undergoes angioplasty; Dr. Breit thinks of Rabbit as "a pretty tough-minded guy with a fair amount of intellectual curiosity" and allows Rabbit to watch the whole procedure on television; Rabbit feels his body is invaded;

2. In the evening Rabbit meets the nurse Annabelle Byer, daughter of his former lover Ruth; Rabbit thinks she is his daughter, "though Ruth out of spite would never admit to it."

1. Reference to Oprah Winfrey's television show;

2. Reference to Michelle Pfeiffer.

## MAY 13, 1989—SATURDAY

1. Janice visits Rabbit at the hospital;

2. Rabbit is jealous of Charlie Stavros, who has been spending some time with Janice helping her out of the present difficulties;

1. Reference to television shows *The Cosby Show, Perfect Strangers, Golden Girls, Roseanne*;

2. Reference to Frank Sinatra and Wayne Newton;

3. Janice informs Rabbit that she fired Lyle, her language full of prejudice against gays;

4. Janice informs Rabbit that his sister Mim, who lives in Las Vegas, called;

5. Rabbit perceives Janice's busyness and determination as a result of her women's group meetings she attended in Florida; as Janice prepares to leave, Rabbit perceives her "black leather pocketbook packed like a bomb . . . that terrorists smuggle into suitcases in airplanes"; before she leaves, he reminds her that the carpets in their house need cleaning.

### MAY 14, 1989—SUNDAY

1. Dr. Breit visits Rabbit and tells him that the angioplasty was only a partial success, that his right coronary artery shows about 80 percent blockage, and that Rabbit may have suffered a postoperative MI;

2. Dr. Breit calls angioplasty a "Mickey-mouse treatment" and wants Rabbit to seriously consider going ahead with a

1. Reference to the tabloid *National Enquirer*;

2. Reference to the film *Witness* and the actress Kelly McGillis.

CABG—the difference in the two procedures is likened to "scrubbing out your toilet bowl with a long brush [or] actually replacing the pipes";

3. Mim calls from Las Vegas; she tells Rabbit that women become "invisible" to men at her age (she is fifty).

### MAY 15, 1989—MONDAY EVENING

1. Rabbit is depressed at the hospital (Janice hasn't come to visit and her classes have started; the day is cloudy, and he hasn't had a bowel movement since he entered the hospital three days ago); he looks in vain at the buildings across the street, hoping to see a woman undressing or coming to the window to look out;

2. Conversation between Rabbit and Ruth's daughter, nurse Annabelle Byer; she tells him that Ruth will be at the hospital and asks him if she should invite her to come up and see him;

3. Rabbit thinks of Ruth, their love affair, and how rude

Ruth was when he wanted to know if Annabelle was his daughter; he decides he doesn't want to see Ruth just now.

## MAY 16, 1989—TUESDAY EVENING

1. Janice visits Rabbit in the hospital and tells him that things at the lot are worse than they thought; they owe "thousands and thousands" of dollars, all money spent to support Nelson's addiction and Lyle's need of expensive medicine;

2. Janice tells him that Nelson has "agreed to enter a rehab place. Immediately";

3. Janice leaves the hospital to "talk things through" with their friend Charlie. Rabbit is jealous and thinks that "he preferred her incompetent";

4. Ronnie Harrison and his wife Thelma (Rabbit's lover) visit him at the hospital;

5. Thelma tells him that she is tired of fighting her disease; claims she can handle the pain

1. More on the Dalai Lama;

2. Reference to television channels AMC, NIK, DSC, PBS;

3. Reference to television shows *Smithsonian World, World of Survival, War and Peace in the Nuclear Age, Nature's Way, Portraits of Power, Wonders of the World, Wildlife Chronicles, Living Body,* and *Planet Earth*;

4. Reference to Sir Laurence Olivier narrating a World War II film clip;

5. Gorbachev visiting China;

6. Students protesting in Tiananmen Square;

7. Reference to George Bush, Barbara Bush, and Ronald Reagan;

8. Reference to Connie

but not the demoralization of the kidneys going: "It takes away your pleasure in life";

6. Rabbit and Ronnie briefly discuss the insurance business.

Chung and Diane Sawyer;

9. Reference to Tom Brokaw;

10. Reference to S and L banks scandal;

11. Reference to Watergate and Richard Nixon's appeal to the nation to turn down their thermostats.

## MAY 17, 1989—WEDNESDAY

1. Nelson leaves at 9:00 A.M. for the rehabilitation clinic, after berating his parents for their past behavior;

2. Rabbit leaves hospital at noon and, because of Janice's test that night, is taken to Nelson's home, where Pru is supposed to take care of him;

3. Rabbit takes a walk and eats a whole bag of corn chips;

4. Janice studies in the afternoon and takes a quiz at 7:00 P.M.; she says she will be back around 10:30 P.M., if they "decide to go out for beers afterward";

5. Rabbit and Pru, alone in the bedroom, talk about Nelson's addiction and their diffi-

1. Reference to television shows *Unsolved Mysteries, thirtysomething, Today, The Cosby Show, Jeopardy, Simon & Simon,* and *Cheers;*

2. Reference to Robert Stack;

3. Reference to Bryant Gumbel and Willard Scott;

4. Reference to Peter Jennings;

5. Reference to Phylicia Rashad;

6. Reference to Michael Jordan;

7. Reference to Jacques Cousteau;

8. Reference to Angela Lansbury;

9. Reference to Greer Gar-

culties; Pru tells Rabbit that she "thought Nelson would grow into somebody like [him]" and that she has wasted her life;

6. Rabbit and Pru make love.

son;

10. Reference to China and Gorbachev;

11. Reference to Governor Casey of Pennsylvania;

12. Reference to film *Dumbo*, *The Sound of Music*, *Dirty Dancing*;

13. Reference to *Consumer Digest*.

## JUNE 19, 1989—MONDAY

1. We learn that Rabbit, now running the lot, went to two family therapy sessions and, feeling discarded and aggravated, decided not to continue;

2. At the lot, Rabbit tells Benny Leone he "did a cookout for everybody on the outdoor grill" for Father's Day;

3. Benny, Rabbit, and Elvira talk about baseball, and Rabbit comments about the absence of loyalty and how Schmidt "in this day and age . . . put honor over money" by retiring;

4. Rabbit says he misses the Cold War, but nobody seems to listen to him;

1. Reference to *Consumer Reports*;

2. Reference to baseball players Steve Bedrosian, Juan Samuel, and Mike Schmidt;

3. Reference to Reagan;

4. Reference to elections in Poland;

5. Reference to Gorbachev;

6. Reference to Chinese government crackdown on students who had been occupying Tiananmen Square;

7. Reference to news of protests in front of abortion clinics by pro-life advocates;

8. Reference to Pope John Paul II;

5. Benny, Rabbit, and Elvira have discussion on abortion, with Elvira taking a pro-choice stand;

6. Rabbit is told by the visiting accountants that from "December to April Brewer Trust extended five car loans to this Angus Barfield, made over to Springer Motors" (according to city records, Angus Barfield had died before Christmas).

9. Reference to George Bush's position on abortion;

10. Reference to Ayatollah Khomeini;

11. Reference to the HUD scandal.

## JULY 4, 1989—TUESDAY

1. Rabbit, having the requisite fair skin, pale blue eyes, and soldierly bearing, is chosen to march as Uncle Sam in a Mount Judge parade; he accepts.

1. Reference to Kate Smith;

2. Reference to greenhouse effect.

## JULY 22, 1989—SATURDAY

1. Rabbit attends Thelma's funeral;

2. Rabbit cannot see Thelma in the minister's description of her;

3. Rabbit meets his old friend Webb Murket and his ex-wife Cindy Murkett;

1. DC-10 crash in Sioux City, Iowa;

2. Reference to the twentieth anniversaries of Woodstock, the Manson Murders, Chappaquidick, and the moon landing.

4. Thelma's children reveal to Rabbit that they, too, at some point tried drugs;

5. At the funeral, Ronnie and Rabbit get into an argument about Thelma; Ronnie tells Rabbit his opinion of their affair: "I don't give a fuck you banged her, what kills me is you did it without giving a shit."

## EARLY AUGUST 1989

1. At 11:00 A.M. Mr. Natsume Shimada, representative of the Toyota Corporation, visits the lot in a limousine;

2. Mr. Shimada, taking Rabbit as synonymous with America, tells him that America's difficulties have to do with the way Americans behave, paying too much attention to freedom and too little attention to order; informs Rabbit that the Toyota franchise is canceled;

3. Rabbit breaks the news of the cancellation to Janice, who has now completed "one pair of ten-week courses" in the

1. More on the greenhouse effect;

2. Reference to Pete Rose;

3. Reference to Oliver North;

4. Reference to film *Parenthood*;

5. Reference to television sitcoms;

6. Reference to the country's debt.

evening;

4. Janice says she is more worried about Rabbit than about Nelson because he doesn't exercise anymore; suggests that he have the bypass;

5. Janice proposes to sell the Florida condo, since she will soon be getting her license and needs to "build local presence";

6. Rabbit gets momentarily excited at the possibility of "rebuilding the lot up from scratch."

## AUGUST 14, 1989—MONDAY

1. Nelson returns from the rehabilitation clinic;

2. Rabbit resents Nelson getting all the attention;

3. Janice tells him they are invited for dinner at Nelson's home tomorrow.

1. Reference to plane crash over Ethiopia, killing black congressman and former Black Panther Mickey Leland;

2. Reference to plane crash which killed white conservative Republican Congressman Larkin Smith;

3. Reference to Mexico's and Brazil's foreign debt;

4. More on the S and L banks scandal.

## AUGUST 15, 1989—TUESDAY

1. Dinner at Nelson's home; Nelson embraces his father and says grace before dinner;

2. Janice presents Nelson's idea of transforming the lot into a drug treatment center, with an eye on government grant money;

3. Rabbit, Janice, and Nelson discuss their debt to Toyota, which has to be paid in two weeks;

4. Janice tells a disappointed Rabbit that Nelson is going back to the lot tomorrow and that she doesn't want him there.

1. Reference to Tom Brokaw;

2. Reference to television evangelists;

3. Reference to Bush's drug war;

4. Reference to FDA's policy towards new drugs for AIDS.

## AUGUST 30, 1989—WEDNESDAY

1. Rabbit and Ronnie play golf at the Flying Eagle;

2. As they play they talk about Voyager's journey past Neptune and about Thelma;

3. As Rabbit arrives at home, the telephone is ringing; Nelson calls to discuss his new deal with Yamaha (instead of cars, they'll sell jet skis, motor-

1. Reference to Voyager 2;

2. Reference to ABC's anchorman Peter Jennings;

3. Reference to George Bush, who is compared to Herbert Hoover;

4. Reference to the Pete Rose settlement.

cycles, trailers, snowmobiles, generators, etc.);

4. Rabbit is told that the debt to Toyota is paid (they got a loan from Brewer Trust by placing a second mortgage on the lot property).

## AUGUST 31, 1989—THURSDAY

1. Janice informs Rabbit that she has decided to sell their house and that they will move in with Nelson and Pru;

2. After dinner, Janice presents her plan to Nelson and Pru; unwilling to accept the idea of having Rabbit and Janice move in with them, Pru decides to tell Janice she and Rabbit have slept together;

3. Janice calls Rabbit to confirm what Pru reveals; he confirms it; Janice calls it "monstrous" and "truly unforgivable" and demands that he come over to Nelson's home to "help undo some of the damage";

4. At 10:07 P.M. Rabbit gets into his Celica and starts driv-

1. Reference to Peter Jennings;

2. Fiftieth anniversary of the beginning of World War II;

3. Reference to Vanna White, of television show *Wheel of Fortune;*

4. Reference to *The Cosby Show;*

5. Reference to Reverend Jim Bakker's trial;

6. Reference to Tammy Bakker, Jim Bakker's wife, and to Jessica Hahn, his secretary;

7. New bomb detector installed at JFK airport;

8. More on PanAm flight 103;

9. Reference to movie *The*

ing to Florida; during the first night he drives as far as Baltimore.

*Freshman,* starring Marlon Brando;

10. Reference to Chancellor Helmut Kohl;

11. Reference to possible CIA complicity in the AIDS epidemic;

12. Reference to Oliver North, Boeski, Milken, Bush, Noriega;

13. Reference to "the missing tritium."

## SEPTEMBER 1, 1989—FRIDAY

1. Rabbit continues driving south, all the way eating high-cholesterol food;

2. In Virginia Rabbit stops for lunch and calls Nelson's home; he talks to Judy and then to Pru and lets her know that he is on his way to their condo in Florida;

3. Rabbit spends the night in Fayetteville, North Carolina.

1. Phillies lost 5 to 1;

2. Bart Giamatti's death;

3. Reference to Pete Rose;

4. Reference to television shows *60 Minutes* and *Perfect Strangers.*

## SEPTEMBER 2, 1989—SATURDAY

1. Rabbit continues his jour-

1. Giamatti's death;

ney towards Florida, the radio on all the time; he listens to easy oldies and news;

2. Rabbit spends his third night at a Ramada Inn beyond Brunswick, Georgia.

2. Reference to HUD;

3. Reference to Montgomery mayor Emory Folmar's prayer march;

4. Reference to other prayer marches in Alabama and Florida;

5. Reference to Jim Bakker;

6. Reference to television shows *The Golden Girls* and *Living Planet*;

7. Reference to Reagan's view of AIDS at the time of Rock Hudson's death;

8. Reference to USS *Vincennes*, which shot down an Iranian civil airliner with over 270 people on board;

9. New Japanese prime minister Toshiki Kaifu meets George Bush in Washington;

10. Reference to provisional government in Panama and the new president of Panama, Francisco Rodriguez;

11. Reference to East Germans in Hungary trying to cross the border.

## SEPTEMBER 3, 1989—SUNDAY

1. Rabbit drives from Brunswick to the condo in Deleon; as he enters Florida he discovers it becomes easier to find stations which play golden oldies;

2. Rabbit reflects on various incidents of his life and how his world has changed since the 1950s;

3. Rabbit arrives at the condo in the middle of the day.

1. Bush's war on drugs speech;

2. The Philadelphia Eagles beat the Miami Dolphins.

## SEPTEMBER 7, 1989—THURSDAY

1. Phone at condo is reconnected;

2. Rabbit calls his home but nobody answers; he talks to very few people, reads the papers, watches television, and reflects on his loneliness;

3. Rabbit makes an appointment with Dr. Morris for September 9.

1. Alarms for Hurricane Gabrielle;

2. Lightning kills a young football player leaving the field after practice in Florida;

3. Hispanic police officer charged with beating his cocker spaniel to death with a crowbar;

4. Sea turtles are dying by the thousands in shrimp nets;

5. Killer named Petit is an-

nounced mentally fit to stand trial;

6. Deion Sanders makes front page of *Fort Myers News-Press*;

7. Boris Becker defeats Ivan Lendl in U.S. open;

8. Reference to television show *Cheers*.

## SEPTEMBER 9, 1989—SATURDAY

1. Rabbit sees Dr. Morris;

2. Dr. Morris tells Rabbit again to keep away from animal fat, television dinners, and "salty junk that comes in bags," to walk several miles a day, and to get interested in something.

1. Reference to Deion Sanders;

2. New York mayor Edward Koch loses Democratic primary elections to black candidate David Dinkins;

3. SAT scores dropping in Lee County;

4. President Bush's appeal to American school children;

5. Mike Schmidt remembered.

## SEPTEMBER 10–17, 1989

1. Rabbit wears his Nikes with a bubble of air and, after digesting the *News-Press*, goes for a walk;

1. Reference to Roy Orbison;

2. Reference to Bart Giamatti;

2. Rabbit walks into black neighborhoods in Deleon, conscious that he is "too white" for the place;

3. Rabbit takes two walks a day, one in the morning and one in late afternoon;

4. Rabbit walks in white neighborhoods;

5. Rabbit receives phone call from Nelson, who tells him that they have an offer for the house, Hyundai is interested in the lot, he and Pru want to have a third child, and that he wants to become a social worker and plans to take a two-year course at the Penn State extension;

6. Rabbit continues to read the history book he started last December.

3. Reference to writer Morgentau's death.

## SEPTEMBER 18, 1989—MONDAY

1. Rabbit ventures several blocks farther into the black neighborhood;

2. Rabbit rests by a dirt basketball court where black kids are playing.

1. Third black Miss America is crowned;

2. Reference to Randall Cunningham's performance in game between the Eagles and the Redskins;

3. Reference to Phylicia

Rashad;

4. Reference to *The Cosby Show*;

5. Reference to Mike Schmidt;

6. Chris Evert plays her last professional tennis game.

### SEPTEMBER 19, 1989—TUESDAY

1. Rabbit walks in the expensive beach-front areas;

2. Rabbit exchanges a few words with laconic and mysterious Mrs. Zabritski;

3. Rabbit continues reading his history book.

1. Hurricane Hugo rips into Puerto Rico.

### SEPTEMBER 20, 1989—WEDNESDAY

1. In the morning Rabbit takes a walk along Pindo Palm Boulevard and brings back a bag of groceries from Winn Dixie;

2. In a kind of trance, Rabbit drives into downtown Deleon and walks to the playing field he discovered yesterday;

3. Rabbit plays a game of Three (horse) with young teen-

1. Hurricane Hugo heading for the United States;

2. Reference to basketball player Michael Jordan;

3. Reference to basketball player Kareem Abdul Jabar;

4. Looting in St. Croix and St. Thomas;

5. Wreckage of French airliner found in the Sahara desert;

agers;

4. Feeling lonely, Rabbit telephones his grandchildren; Pru answers the phone and tells him that Nelson is HIV-negative and that Janice is at their home at that moment celebrating the sale of her first house; Janice refuses to talk to him;

5. Rabbit talks with his grandchildren;

6. After he hangs up, Rabbit eats a fatty double-dinner and reads history.

6. Reference to PanAm flight 103;

7. Reference to anchormen Tom Brokaw (NBC) and Peter Jennings (ABC);

8. Reference to television shows *Growing Pains* and *Unsolved Mysteries*.

## SEPTEMBER 21, 1989—THURSDAY

1. Rabbit reads the *Fort Myers News-Press*;

2. At 10:00 A.M., Rabbit goes for his walk; he drives downtown and walks to black section;

3. Rabbit meets a "lone tall boy in denim cutoffs [who] is shooting baskets by himself";

4. Rabbit invites the black young man to play a one-on-one game to twenty-one;

5. Rabbit suffers a heart at-

1. Hurricane Hugo aims at the southeastern United States;

2. USAir jet crashes in New York river;

3. Bomb announced as probable cause of crash of French DC-10 over the Sahara;

4. Chaos and looting in St. Croix after hurricane passes;

5. Reference to PanAm flight 103.

tack and is left alone on the dirt
court;

6. Approaching sirens are
mistaken for a hurricane alert
by several of the elderly poor.

## SEPTEMBER 22, 1989—FRIDAY

1. Janice and Dr. Olman talk
about Rabbit's chances for survival;

2. Dr. Olman explains that
Rabbit's infarction "looks to be
transmural";

3. Janice reflects about how
difficult it was to take a night
flight to Florida with Eastern
on strike and Hurricane Hugo
closing the Atlanta airport;

4. Janice sees Rabbit; she
forgives him;

5. Nelson talks to Rabbit and
begs him not to die; Rabbit replies, "Well, Nelson, all I can
tell you is, it isn't so bad."

1. Strike at Eastern Air-
lines;

2. Air traffic delays be-
cause of Hurricane Hugo;

3. Hugo clobbers South
Carolina.

OBSERVATION: Mr. Shimada's visit in early August 1989 parallels the
change of government in Japan with the election of Toshikui Kaifu, a liberal
democrat, as prime minister. Kaifu's election and the Socialist Party's impact
upon Japanese-American relations were widely discussed in the media. On
August 9 former trade negotiator Makoto Kurodo expressed concern that the
Japanese might view America more negatively. Prime Minister Kaifu visited
the United States on September 1.

# APPENDIX 2

## WORKS PUBLISHED BY JOHN UPDIKE

1958    *The Carpentered Hen and Other Tame Creatures*
        (poetry).[1]

1959    *The Poorhouse Fair* (novel);
        *The Same Door* (collection of short stories);
        *Hoping for a Hoopoe* (English publication of *The Carpen-
        tered Hen and Other Tame Creatures*).

1960    *Rabbit, Run* (novel).

1962    *Pigeon Feathers and Other Stories* (collection of short
        stories);
        *The Magic Flute* (with Warren Chappell, adapted from
        Wolfgang Amadeus Mozart's *The Magic Flute*).

1963    *The Centaur* (novel);
        *Telephone Poles and Other Poems* (poetry).

---

[1] Except when noted otherwise, all books were published by Alfred Knopf.

1964   *The Ring* (with Warren Chappell, adapted  from libretto
          by Richard Wagner).

1965   *Of the Farm* (novel);
          *The Carpentered Hen and Other Tame Cretures/ Tele-   phone
          Poles and Other Poems* (poetry);
          *The Poorhouse Fair* (novel);
          *Assorted Prose* (essays);
          *A Child's Calendar* (juvenile poetry).

1966   *The Music School* (collection of short stories).

1968   *Couples* (novel);
          *The Angels* (poetry); Pensacola: King and Queen Press;
          *On Meeting Authors*  (essay) Newburyport: Wickford;
          *Three Texts from Early Ipswich* (historical pageant).

1969   *Midpoint and Other Poems* (poetry).

1970   *Bech: A Book* (short novel).

1971   *Rabbit Redux* (novel).

1972   *Seventy Poems* (poetry). New York: Penguin.

1973   *Six Poems* (poetry). Oliphant Press;
          *Warm Wine: An Idyll* (short story) New York: Albondon-
             cani Press.
          *A Good Place: Being a Personal Account of Ipswich, Mas-
             sachusetts.* New York: Aloe Editions.

1974   *Cunts* (poetry). Frank Hallman;
       *Buchanan Dying* (play).

1975   *A Month of Sundays* (novel);
       *Picked-up Pieces* (essays).

1976   *Marry Me: A Romance* (novel);
       "Couples: A Short Story" (short story). Cambridge: Halty
              Ferguson. .

1977   *Tossing and Turning* (poetry);
       "Hub Fans Bid Kid Adieu" (essay). Northridge: Lord John.

1978   *The Coup* (novel);
       "From The Journal of a Leper" (short story). Northridge:
              Lord John;
       Introduction to Henry Green's book *Loving, Living, Party
              Going*. Penguin.

1979   *Sixteen Sonnets* (poetry). Cambridge:  Halty Ferguson;
       *Problems and Other Stories* (short stories);
       *Too Far to Go: The Maple Stories* (short stories). Fawcett;
       *Three Illuminations in the Life of an American Author*   (short
       story). New York: Targ;
       "Talk from the Fifties" (essay). Northridge: Lord John;
       Introduction to Bruno Schultz's *Sanatorium under the
              Sign of  the Hourglass*. Penguin.

1980   *Five Poems* (poetry). Cleveland: Bits Press;
       *Your Lover Just Called: Stories of Joan and Richard Maple*
              (short stories). New York: Penguin;
       "The Chaste Planet" (short story). Worcester: Metacom;

*People One Knows: Interviews with Insufficiently Famous*
          *Americans* (short story). Northridge: Lord John;
"Ego and Art in Walt Whitman" (essay). New York: Targ;
Afterword to Edmund Wilson's *Memoirs of Hecate*
          *County*. Boston: Nonpareil.

1981    "Hawthorne's Creed" (essay). New York: Targ;
          *Rabbit is Rich* (novel).

1982    *Spring Trio* (poetry). Winston-Salem: Palaemon Press;
          "More Stately Mansions: A Story" (short story). Jackson:
                    Nouveau Press;
          *Bech is Back* (short story).

1983    *Hugging the Shore: Essays and Criticism* (essays).

1984    *The Witches of Eastwick* (novel);
          *Jester's Dozen* (poetry). Northridge: Lord John;
          *Confessions of a Wild Bore* (short story). Newton: Tama-
                    zunchale Press;
          "Emersonianism" (essay). Cleveland: Bits Press.

1985    *Facing Nature: Poems* (poetry).

1986    *Roger's Version* (novel).

1987    *Trust Me: Short Stories* (short stories).

1988    *S.* (novel).

1989    *Just Looking: Essays on Art* (essays);
          *Self-Consciousness: Memoirs* (memoirs).

1990    *Rabbit at Rest* (novel).

1991    *Odd Jobs: Essays and Criticism* (essays);
        Introduction to Magnum Photos, *Heroes and Anti-heroes*.
                New York: Random House.

1992    *Memories of the Ford Administration* (novel).

1993    *Collected Poems: 1953–1993* (poetry);
        *Concerts at Castle Hill* (essays). Northridge: Lord John.

1994    *Brazil* (novel);
        *A Helpful Alphabet of Friendly Objects* (poetry);
        *The Afterlife and Other Stories* (short stories).

1995    *Rabbit Angstrom: The Four Novels* (Rabbit tetralogy).

1996    *In the Beauty of the Lilies* (novel);
        *Golf Dream: Writings on Golf* (essays);
        Introduction to Edith Wharton's *The Age of Innocence*.
                New York: Ballantine.

1997    *Toward the End of Time* (novel).

# Appendix 3

## Prizes Won By John Updike

1959   Guggenheim Fellowship in poetry;

1960   American Academy and National Institute of Arts and
Letters;
Rosenthal Foundation Award for *The Poorhouse Fair;*

1963   National Book Award in fiction for *The Centaur;*

1964   National Book Award;
Elected to the National Institute of Arts and Letters;

1966   Prix Medicis Etranger for *The Centaur;*
O. Henry Award in fiction for "The Bulgarian
Poetess";

1972   Fulbright Fellow in Africa;

1977   Member of American Academy of Arts and Letters;

1979   New England Poetry Club Golden Rose;

1980   American Book Award nomination for *Too Far to Go:
The Maple Stories;*

1981   Edward MacDowell Medal for literature;

1982    Pulitzer Prize in fiction for *Rabbit Is Rich*;
American Book Award for *Rabbit Is Rich*;
National Book Critics Circle Award in fiction for *Rabbit Is Rich*;
Union League Club Abraham Lincoln Award;

1984    National Book Critics Circle Award in criticism for *Hugging the Shore*;
Medal of Honor for literature, National Arts Club of New York City;

1986    National Book Critics Circle Award in fiction nomination for *Roger's Version*;
PEN/Malamud Memorial Prize, PEN/ Faulkner Award Foundation, for excellence in short story writing;

1989    National Medal of Arts;

1990    Pulitzer Prize for *Rabbit at Rest*;
National Book Critics Award for *Rabbit at Rest*;

1991    Premio Scanno;

1995    Howells Medal, American Academy of Arts and Letters;

1996    Ambassador Book Award for *In the Beauty of the Lilies*;

1997    *Commandeur de l'Ordre des Arts et des Lettres.*

# INDEX

# MODERN AMERICAN LITERATURE
## New Approaches

*Yoshinobu Hakutani, General Editor*

The books in this series deal with many of the major writers known as American realists, modernists, and post-modernists from 1880 to the present. This category of writers will also include less known ethnic and minority writers, a majority of whom are African American, some are Native American, Mexican American, Japanese American, Chinese American, and others. The series might also include studies on well-known contemporary writers, such as James Dickey, Allen Ginsberg, Gary Snyder, John Barth, John Updike, and Joyce Carol Oates. In general, the series will reflect new critical approaches such as deconstructionism, new historicism, psychoanalytical criticism, gender criticism/feminism, and cultural criticism.

For additional information about this series or for the submission of manuscripts, please contact:

Peter Lang Publishing
Acquisitions Department
516 N. Charles St., 2nd Floor
Baltimore, MD 21201